STAN LEE

Stan Lee

A Life in Comics

LIEL LEIBOVITZ

Yale

UNIVERSITY

PRESS

New Haven and London

Frontispiece: Stan Lee, 1996. Evan Hurd Photography,
Corbis Historical Collection, Getty Images.

Yale University Press books may be purchased in quantity for educational,
business, or promotional use. For information, please e-mail sales.press@yale.edu
(U.S. office) or sales@yaleup.co.uk (U.K. office).

Set in Janson type by Integrated Publishing Solutions, Grand Rapids, Michigan.
Printed in the United States of America.

Library of Congress Control Number: 2019950942
ISBN 978-0-300-23034-5 (hardcover : alk. paper)

A catalogue record for this book is available from the British Library.

This paper meets the requirements of ANSI/NISO Z39.48-1992
(Permanence of Paper).

10 9 8 7 6 5 4 3 2 1

To Lisa, Lily, and Hudson, my heroes

CONTENTS

1

So What's the Risk?

STAN LEE was ready to quit.

It was the summer of 1961, and the past seven years had been packed with enough drama to fill several of the schlocky comic books he and his colleagues were churning out each week. The troubles began in 1954, when Fredric Wertham, a Bavarian-born psychiatrist and a disciple of Freud's, embarked on an anticomics crusade: he had interviewed scores of juvenile delinquents, he announced in his book—the unimprovably titled *Seduction of the Innocent*—and was shocked to learn they were all avid comics readers. Having little patience for the distinction between correlation and causation, Congress took up Wertham's cause, and—in a series of televised hearings that began the same month as the Army-McCarthy hearings and evoked the same feverish strand of Cold War paranoia—summoned a roster of comic book publishers to chastise them for featuring excessively violent images. Eager to keep on the right side of regulation, the publishers rushed to create the Comics Code Authority, which set strict guidelines of self-censorship. "In every instance," the 1954 code decreed, "good shall triumph over evil and the criminal punished for his misdeeds." Nor could seduction be portrayed, to say nothing of "sex perversion or any inference to same."

The industry's self-imposed piety, however, did little to win it new fans. Years later, Lee recalled striking up a conversation with a gun salesman while spending a weekend in the Catskills and mentioning that he was a comic book editor. "That is absolutely criminal," the man scoffed. "Totally reprehensible. You should go to jail for the crime you're committing."[1] The story, like many of Lee's finest, is probably apocryphal, but the contempt in which many Americans held comic book creators was not. And if that wasn't bad enough, the comic book industry, no longer able to produce popular titles like *Crime SuspenStories* or *Crypt of Terror*, was soon in a tailspin of cutbacks and layoffs. Summoned by his boss one afternoon, Lee was told that the company's production would soon dwindle to just a handful of titles a month, and that he had to fire the entire staff. "It was the toughest thing I did in my life," he'd recall decades later. "I had to tell them, and I was friends with these people. So many of them, I had dinner with them at their homes—I knew their wives, their kids, and I had to tell them this. It was, as I say, the most horrible thing I ever had to do."[2]

Booted from his spacious office, Lee now sat at a small cubicle in the company's profitable men's magazine division, spending his days working on anodyne stuff like the foibles of two models named Millie and Chili or the adventures of a diaper-wearing dragon. He'd been with the company, which started as Timely Comics and was now called Atlas, since 1939, and had risen rapidly through its ranks—from inkwell filler and sandwich fetcher to editor in chief—but now he was beginning to think the business was moribund. "It's like a ship sinking," he confided in a colleague, "and we're the rats. And we've got to get off."[3]

But getting off meant risking unemployment, and that Lee just couldn't do. Growing up, he'd come home from school each day and watch his father, a fabric cutter in the Garment District robbed of his livelihood by the Great Depression, sit at the kitchen table and stare blankly into space. With a wife and a small child to care for, Lee could think of no fate more terrifying than replaying the central drama of his childhood, which centered on his parents bickering about money. Unhappy, he tried to dream up other ways of making a living, such as self-publishing a book of photographs with humorous captions or trying to sell a TV script. There was one brief glimmer of hope in 1958, when he and a friend, the artist Joe Maneely, sold an independent newspaper comic strip called *Mrs. Lyons' Cubs*, about a Scouting den mother and her gaggle of wisecracking boys, but it, too, was doomed: having lost his glasses, and having had a little bit to drink, Maneely stepped out between two train cars to get some fresh air on his commute back home to New Jersey one evening and fell to his death.

Lee soldiered on for a few more years, but each day his view of the industry grew dimmer. He was never a comic book fanatic—as a child, he read Dickens and Twain, not Superman and Batman—and he was beginning to wonder whether the genre he'd spent twenty years writing and editing was just a passing fad. And even if it wasn't, did he really want to spend the rest of his life coming up with story lines about creatures named Groot, Droom, or Krang? Nearing forty, Lee wanted to write something that mattered, real stories about complicated people who struggled with a range of emotions you couldn't show when all you did was comics. Getting his start in the business, he took on the moniker Stan Lee, keeping his real name—Stanley Martin Lieber—for that great American novel he'd always intended to write. Maybe, he thought, maybe it was time to get serious.

The thought recurred with particular urgency one day when his boss, Martin Goodman, came back from a round of golf and summoned Lee to his office. He'd just played with the publisher of DC Comics, Jack Liebowitz, he told Lee, and he learned that DC was making a mint from a new series called the Justice League. The idea was simple: rather than showcase just one superhero, DC decided to throw all its eggs in one basket, drafting Superman, Batman, Wonder Woman, the Flash, and others into one megatitle. It was selling like hotcakes, Liebowitz told Goodman, who rushed back to work and ordered his editor to come up with a knockoff that could also do some brisk business.

It was the last thing Lee wanted to hear. When he got back home that evening, he told his wife, Joanie, about his conversation with Goodman. She asked him what he said, and Lee sighed. "I said I'd think about it," he replied, "but really, what's the point? I don't want to just keep recycling old characters." Then, after a pause, he admitted out loud what had, until then, been nothing more than a dark thought: "I feel like quitting."

Joanie was silent for a moment. "Look, Stan," she finally said, "if you want to quit, you know I'll support you. But think about this: If Martin wants you to create a new group of superheroes, this could be the chance for you to do it the way you've always wanted to. You could dream up plots that have more depth and substance to them, and create characters that have interesting personalities, who speak like real people." It could be fun, she said, to experiment a bit; besides, she added with a smile, "the worst that can happen is that Martin gets mad and fires you. But you want to quit anyway, so what's the risk?"[4]

Convinced, Lee got to work. He had no concrete ideas. What he did have was a list of resentments, compiled over two decades of watching the industry produce titles he considered derivative or worse.

First, there was the matter of the superhero himself. Never a big fan of Superman, the prototypical comic book protagonist, Lee saw no point to a story about a character who was, by definition, infallible. In his very first issue, in the summer of 1938, Superman saved a wrongfully accused woman from the electric chair, taught an abusive husband a painful lesson, saved an abducted Lois Lane by picking up her kidnappers' car with his bare hands, and stopped a treasonous senator from starting a war with Europe, all in thirteen pages and without once breaking a sweat. Sure, he was, as his creators advertised on the comic book's last page, "a physical marvel, a mental wonder" who was "destined to reshape the destiny of the world!" But was he interesting? Lee wasn't sure. The heroes he'd grown up admiring were different: Sherlock Holmes was a cocaine-addled misanthrope who could not be trusted to live on his own and whose mental state was of constant concern to his friends; Quasimodo was a hunchback driven to murder; Hamlet was best remembered for contemplating whether or not life itself was worth the trouble. Why, then, did comic book heroes have to be so uniform in their bland goodness? Couldn't they afford the occasional fit of rage or moment of anguish? Did they not, on occasion, make terrible mistakes? And why did they always insist on keeping their identity secret? If I had any superpower, Lee often thought to himself, I'd like everyone in the world to know about it.

Just as inane as the hero was the sidekick. Lee understood why the industry delivered so many bright-eyed young foils, from Batman's Robin to Superman's Jimmy Olsen: without them, the omnipotent caped machos would do little but fly, punch, lift, and strut, silent save for the occasional awkward soliloquy. But throw in a young charge, and suddenly the hero, in a paternal mood, feels compelled to narrate his actions and wax poetic about the dangers at hand. And if the youth just happens to be about the same age as the average comic reader, all the better. Lee understood this dynamic well, but he found it infantilizing. Readers, he believed, even young ones, were smart enough to figure out the plot by themselves, and, besides, all this explicating made superheroes seem more like middle school teachers than masked avengers.

But the boys, at least, got a taste of crime fighting; women had no such privilege. Unlike Superman, Lois Lane was confined to falling: in love, into trouble, and off of tall buildings, flailing her arms for her hero to save her. Sure, there were a handful of exceptional heroines, like Wonder Woman or Batwoman, but they were anomalies, interesting precisely because you didn't expect to see a woman suit up and join the men in their games. Which limited any writer, Lee thought, in two ways: it meant you could tell stories only about men, and also that these men were doomed to be in cardboard relationships that looked and felt nothing like the nurturing and demanding marriage Lee himself was enjoying with Joanie, a partnership between two thoughtful and loving adult human beings.

And, finally, there was the question of how the comic books themselves were created. In a compartmentalized industry in which each artisan—the writer, the penciler, the inker, the colorist—was expected to do his or her bit and nothing more, Lee already had a reputation for pioneering a method that left much room for improvisation; he presented his artists with a detailed synopsis of the plot, jumping on his desk and acting out a scene here and there when the occasion called for it, but then let them draw whatever they saw fit before receiving their pages and filling in the text. It was the same principle that was already making The Second City theater in Chicago, established two years earlier, famous: bring a couple of creative people together, throw in a clearly defined premise, and let each of them riff on and feed off the other to receive a whole that was somehow larger than the sum of its parts.

This being Lee's last-ditch effort, there was only one man he trusted enough to make the most of this game of improvisation. He dashed off a memo with a few ideas for characters and handed it to a short man who chomped on Roi-Tan cigars and worked fourteen-hour days, delivering four or five inventive and complete pages in the time it took other artists to complete a draft of one. If anyone could make something of his crazy idea, he told his wife, it was Jack Kirby.

For two Jewish boys who were born five years apart and grew up within a few miles of each other in New York City, Lee and Kirby were a study in opposites. Lee had spent his childhood reading the classics and dreaming of becoming a celebrated novelist; Kirby spent his fist-fighting in a street gang and dreaming of making it through the day without getting too badly beaten up. Lee was charming and animated, speaking in full sentences gilded with exclamation marks; words left Kirby's mouth with some difficulty, squeezing past the baleen of his thick Lower East Side accent. Lee was five feet, eleven inches, and athletic; Kirby was much smaller and stooped, a curvature shaped by long hours of being hunched over his drawing desk. When they first met, decades earlier, Kirby had been the industry's brightest star—having just released a comic book featuring his newest creation, Captain America, socking it to Adolf Hitler—and Lee was his teenaged assistant. But Lee was now the one calling the shots. Like every other comic artist at the time, Kirby owned none of his characters and was paid a pittance per page. It was reason enough to resent Lee, management's errand boy. But even a tough guy like Kirby couldn't deny that as annoying and loquacious as Lee could sometimes be, he had great ideas.

Precisely how Lee approached Kirby with his Hail Mary for a genre-defying new comic book is a matter of unresolved dispute. Some, including Lee himself, argue that Lee had jotted down a feverish four-page memo, complete with all the characters and the basic plotline, and handed it to Kirby to draw. Others, including Kirby, hold that the two men had a chat, came up with the characters together, and then set out to work, with Lee summarizing their ideas in his memo and Kirby getting busy designing the new heroes and their world. Whatever happened, you had only to read the first four pages of their new collaboration to understand that it was not only a joint creation but a fictionalized yet emotionally resonant portrayal of their relationship.

The role of Lee was played by the character Reed Richards. Exposed to cosmic rays while on a rogue mission to Mars—the space race and fear of nuclear radiation both being popular preoccupations of the time—Richards crashes back to Earth only to discover that he can stretch and twist his body in whichever way he chooses. With Lee's sense of hyperbole, Richards names himself Mister Fantastic.

"There had been a comic book a million years ago called Plastic Man," Lee told an interviewer decades later. "And the character could stretch. But it was a humorous type of thing, but I always felt that would be great for a serious hero. So I thought I'll give our hero the ability to stretch. But not wanting him just to be a copy of something, I felt he'll also be the greatest, smartest scientist on the face of the earth. And to make him, again, not a cliché, not a typical guy, I figured he'll be the most boring human being in the world, a little bit like me. He talks too much, he uses big words, and the others, especially the Thing, will always be saying 'will you shut up!'"[5]

The Thing would be Ben Grimm, Richards's pilot and a stand-in for Jack Kirby, looking and sounding just like the artist. Grimm's trip to space isn't as auspicious as that of his nemesis: instead of gaining elasticity, he's transformed into a stony mass of a man, a walking crater that can fold a thick sheet of metal without trying too hard. Ineloquent and brooding, the Thing comes to life only when practicing his craft—lifting, smashing, pounding, clobbering—or when butting heads with Mr. Fantastic. Two other members were thrown into the mix as well: Susan Storm, Richards's fiancée, whom the groovy space rays turn into the Invisible Girl, and her brother Johnny, a hot-headed teenager endowed with the ability to spontaneously combust and turn himself into the fast-flying Human Torch. Together, they were called the Fantastic Four.

In those days, sales figures took months to tabulate, but Martin Goodman didn't need to wait for a balance sheet to know that Lee had given him a hit. The company's mail room was soon awash in letters, not the usual missives from cranky readers complaining about missing staples but passionate notes from eloquent fans who found much to love about the newest stars in the comics constellation. Speaking of stars, the cosmos itself seemed to smile on Lee's conceit: shortly after the first issue was completed but before it went to print, a diminutive Russian colonel named Yuri Gagarin shouted *poyekhali*—Russian for "let's go"—before blasting off aboard *Vostok 1* and orbiting planet Earth once, an hour and forty-eight–minute–long journey that made him the first human being ever to travel to outer space. Americans, taken aback by the sudden Soviet dominance, were ready for astronauts of their own, even fictional ones who bickered all the time and seemed as interested in their own insecurities as they were in the planet's. Moved by the reactions he was getting, Lee scrapped any plans of retirement, throwing his all into the new series. By the third issue, he felt optimistic enough to slap an unrestrained tagline on every new Fantastic Four comic book published: "The Greatest Comic Magazine in the World!!"

Quickly, Goodman canceled a lumbering title, *Teen-Age Romance*, and instructed Lee to deliver another hero: the Hulk arrived in May 1962, followed, in August, by both Spider-Man and Thor. Iron Man debuted the following March, and by the time 1963, the grievous year of the Kennedy assassination, slouched to an end, Lee, almost always working with Kirby, had delivered Doctor Strange, the X-Men, and the Avengers. By the end of the decade, the Silver Surfer, the Black Panther, and the Guardians of the Galaxy had all joined the pantheon.

It would be wise, in considering the legacy of an effervescent self-promoter like Stan Lee, to watch out for overstatement, but there's none of it in the argument that Lee's creations redefined America's sense of itself. By any measure of significance at our disposal, few artists have had so much of an impact on American popular culture: no sooner do you tally up the billions of dollars his characters have raked in at the multiplex than a new sequel comes along, dominating not only the box office but the conversation as well. It is not uncommon to try to make sense of our contemporaries by trying to figure out where they would fit in the fictional universe Lee created, telling ourselves, for example, that a certain unstable billionaire inventor is our real-life Iron Man or that a combative and thin-skinned president is like Thanos, the Avengers' nemesis. These analogies aren't just lazy shorthand or, like some nearsighted critics argue, a sign of a generation wading in shallow cultural waters; they're an indication of how deeply ingrained Lee's work has become in our collective imagination, and of just how much of that collective imagination it occupies. Generations of Americans who had lost the facility to talk and think about moral issues—about good versus evil, about power and responsibility—a domain once reserved exclusively for the church, the mosque, and the synagogue, rediscovered it in Lee's work. It was this contribution to the reawakening of America's moral imagination that President George W. Bush had in mind when he awarded Lee the National Medal of the Arts in 2008. "His complex plots and humane super heroes," read the medal's citation, "celebrate courage, honesty, and the importance of helping the less fortunate, reflecting America's inherent goodness."

And yet, while Lee's contributions to the culture have been hailed loudly and often, his ideas remain largely unexplored. In part, it's because many of us still approach comics like that snobby salesman who spurned Lee all those decades ago, refusing to believe that the slim, illustrated volumes can contain depths worth excavating. Sadly, even the scholarly study of comics, now a cottage industry, frequently succumbs to this assumption, focusing on history and sociology but rarely on philosophy and theology. We may speak of Lee's work in religious terms like "inherent goodness," but when we attempt to understand it, we think of it at best as a makeshift modern mythology and at worst as an adult projection of childish fantasies.

That disdain, too, is like something straight out of a Stan Lee comic book. While the first issue of *The Fantastic Four* heralded the quartet's arrival, the second already had them on the defensive, misunderstood and mistrusted by the very people they were toiling to save. Anyone with even a hint of familiarity with the Bible would recognize the pattern of the flawed and conflicted leaders wrestling with their stiff-necked people.

Which isn't to suggest that we ought to read Mister Fantastic strictly as a latter-day Moses, or the Silver Surfer as another Abraham, or Spider-Man as the reincarnation of Cain. Literary comparisons, especially ones involving scriptures, are instructive only when used as signposts, not blueprints. Nor is it particularly helpful to turn to Lee himself in search of exegesis; like many of the greats, he let his work do the arguing, and confined himself to the sort of cryptic statements that served only to invite further inquiry. Anyone looking for definitive evidence that Lee's pantheon of heroes amounts to more than a few misfits in tights locked in endless battle is likely to walk away disappointed. But anyone looking for definitive evidence is probably not interested in comic books anyway: more than any other art form, perhaps, comics is an interpreter's medium, delivering a succession of icons, as cryptic as they are canonic, and inviting the reader to weave them into the larger stories of his or her life. To truly grapple with the Thing or the Hulk, to make sense of Thor or the X-Men, to learn from Professor Xavier or Doctor Doom, we need to understand these characters as they were always intended to be understood, as creations animated by the spirit that has always animated America's emotional life, a spirit that used to reside in houses of worship before circumstances drove it to seek refuge elsewhere, in rock 'n' roll music, in comic books, in the flotsam of popular culture. We also need to read them as characters formed by the anxieties of first-generation American Jews who had fought in World War II, witnessed the Holocaust, and reflected—consciously or otherwise—on the moral obligations and complications of life after Auschwitz. In many ways, the story of our current scrum of superheroes is the story of what we've come to believe and why, and it begins in a small apartment on the Upper West Side of Manhattan, on the precipice of the Great Depression.

2

Stan Lee Is God

THINGS WERE LOOKING UP for Jack Lieber. It had hardly been two decades since he and his brother had washed up on Ellis Island, two teenagers seeking refuge. Jack, then known as Hyman, was nineteen; Abraham was fourteen. They did not come to America, like many other immigrants at the time, in search of economic opportunity. They came to escape their newly independent homeland, Romania, which was celebrating its sovereignty by barring Jews from public schools and universities, making them take humiliating oaths in court, and, when all else failed, launching old-fashioned murderous pogroms. In New York, the brothers found work in the garment industry, and, impoverished, lived as boarders with a string of Jewish families who had rooms to let and needed the cash.

The older Lieber worked hard, eventually distinguishing himself as a skilled fabric cutter. In his spare time, he frequented the cafés on the Lower East Side, where his *landsleit* lingered, eating dishes that reminded them of home and catching up on the latest gossip. By 1920, Jack Lieber, thirty-four years old, had enough money and enough confidence to test out the American dream. He proposed to Celia Solomon, another Romanian immigrant, and moved to a large apartment on West 98th Street and West End Avenue. Two years later, on December 28, 1922, their first son, Stanley Martin Lieber—better known by the moniker he would soon embrace, Stan Lee—was born.

In numerous interviews and autobiographies, Lee, ever the bubbly optimist, painted his childhood as mostly cheerful, a string of days spent reading classic books and exploring New York on his bike. "When I rode it," he waxed poetic, "in my imagination I was a mighty knight atop a noble steed. That bike was my best friend because it gave me a feeling of freedom. . . . I could ride all over the city, go wherever I pleased. No kid ever loved a bike more than I loved mine."[1] Lee was also active in the drama club of the local synagogue his family attended regularly, though whether that suggested a passion for reenacting the stories of the Bible or being close to a certain young lady he liked remains unclear. But his exploits on two wheels and on stage may very well have been a means of escape: Before Lee had turned seven, the stock market crashed, plunging the nation into the Great Depression.

At first, Jack Lieber remained resilient. He had spent too many years clawing his way into the middle class to lose heart. When he could no longer find work cutting cloth, he withdrew all of the family's life savings and, figuring that even in tough economic times people had to eat, bought a diner. It flopped, leaving Jack penniless. He moved his family to a smaller apartment in Washington Heights, but in 1931 he and Celia welcomed another boy, Larry, into their family, their meager resources now stretched even thinner. Soon, the Liebers moved again, this time to a railroad flat in the Bronx. Unable to afford a phone, Jack left the house each morning to look for work in person, and returned each afternoon, empty-handed. Lee would watch him just sitting there at the kitchen table, not knowing where to find the money for the family's next meal or next month's rent.

The tension made Lee's parents quarrel, and the quarrels sent him looking for distractions. Books were his favorite source of entertainment, as was the radio—for an hour on Sunday nights, between 8 and 9 P.M., Lee, his brother, and his parents gathered in the living room and listened to *The Chase and Sanborn Hour*, which featured the period's biggest stars, including Eddie Cantor, Jimmy Durante, W. C. Fields, Walter Winchell, Nelson Eddy, Mae West, and, Lee's favorite, the ventriloquist Edgar Bergen. A ventriloquist's act naturally loses much of its dazzle when performed on the radio, where no one could see whether Bergen's lips were moving or not, but the entertainer made up for the medium's shortcomings by endowing his wooden dummy, Charlie McCarthy, with sharp and irreverent wit. Charlie was particularly fond of trading insults with W. C. Fields, whom he derided as a no-good drunk:

> FIELDS: Tell me, Charles, is it true that your father was a gate-leg table?
>
> CHARLIE: If it is, your father was under it.[2]

Lee, who was always moved by the rhythms of language, was overjoyed by such banter. He loved Shakespeare's cadences, but the puppet's were much faster, and could be applied as weapons—razor-sharp barbs that could cut even an acerbic movie star earning five thousand dollars per week. Lee took a similar pleasure in Errol Flynn, whom he'd watch whenever he could afford a ticket to the palatial Loew's theater on 175th Street in Washington Heights, relishing the actor's playful disdain for authority—as Robin Hood, as Captain Blood—and the joy with which he leapt, often literally, into action.

And then there were the funnies. Long before Superman

put on his cape and dashed off to champion the needy, dozens of newspapers competed for readership by publishing a bevy of recurring strips targeting the less affluent and less educated. Among Lee's favorites were Dick Tracy and his gallery of homicidal nemeses, and the Katzenjammer Kids, two German brothers who found their life's meaning in tormenting the handful of adults unfortunate enough to care for them, particularly der Captain, their surrogate father, and der Inspector, the representative of the local school system entrusted with attempting to improve the two imps. "Mit dese kids," went der Inspector's battle cry, "society iss nix!"

It was more than just a humorous catchphrase. The damage the Great Depression had wrought on the nation's economy was easily measurable in terrifying numbers, like 24, the percentage of Americans unemployed by 1932. But society is a more complicated construct, held together by shared affinities and emotional currents. And society, by the time Lee was old enough to notice it, seemed poised to implode. "Hoover," the writer Caroline Bird noted, "chose the word 'Depression' in 1929 because it sounded less frightening than 'panic' or 'crisis,' the words that had formerly been used for economic downturns," but the term proved grimly apt at capturing the way scarcity "hurt people and maimed them permanently because it literally depressed mind and spirit."[3] And while the depredations of want on the mind were warded off individually, its attacks on the spirit were experienced collectively. Writing in the darkest point of the Depression, William Kelley Wright, a philosopher teaching at Dartmouth College, observed that "today we are passing through a period of religious depression not less severe than the concomitant moral and economic depression."[4] He was hardly being hyperbolic. In 1905, a survey querying Americans about traditional Christianity learned, to no one's surprise, that 78 percent of respondents viewed the nation's predominant faith favorably; by 1930, the number had dropped to 33 percent.[5]

In part, the decline was probably a response to the worsening conditions of life, the cri de coeur of a traditionally faithful nation feeling momentarily abandoned by Providence. But the tailspin of belief, as the theologian Reinhold Niebuhr noted in his first book, published in 1927, was equally propelled by the dueling forces that have forever been present in the machinations of American life: fundamentalism on the one hand, and modernism on the other. The fight between these two forces unfurled as government agencies came along and, under the auspices of the New Deal, offered the sort of financial aid and relief previously delivered exclusively by churches and synagogues. Unable to provide balm of any kind to the ravages of the Great Depression, communities of faith in all corners of America dug in their heels and, in many cases, promoted increasingly fantastical responses to the crisis, with many insisting that the economic disaster was nothing but a divine test that, once passed, would usher in an era of unparalleled prosperity. Not surprisingly, it was a theology most congregants had difficulty embracing.

Focused primarily on his family's well-being, Lee observed none of these cataclysmic clashes. But as an avid consumer of popular culture, he saw them replayed everywhere. What, for example, was Dick Tracy if not a herald of modernism, charging forth, with the latest forensic technology at his disposal, to defeat the demonic forces of unreason that imperiled America's progress? And who were the Katzenjammer Kids if not merry fundamentalists, unleashing the spirit against a gaggle of grown-ups insistent on imposing order with their rules and regulations? The funnies delivered a raucous version of Garry Wills's observation that the nation was forever pulled in different directions by its head and its heart, the former embodied by the elites and their scientific-minded Enlightenment values and the latter by the same folks who sat in on tent revivals and yearned for redemption, and that if it had any prayer of moving forward it could do so only by getting these two organs to work together.

The best way to do that, of course, was by committing both head and heart to sheer action in service of some greater cause, as had happened, say, when ecstatic laymen gathered under the leadership of skeptical officers during the Revolutionary War. Action soon emerged as a preoccupation of Lee's; increasingly, he sought entertainment that delivered its ideas not in long and considered paragraphs but in short kinetic bursts. Charles William Kahles's *Hairbreadth Harry* became one of his favorite cartoon strips: the hero, a strapping and unflappable fair-haired lad, courted the Beautiful Belinda Blinks while fending off the devious schemes of Relentless Rudolph Ruddigore Rassendale. Unlike the other strips Lee enjoyed, *Harry* wasn't allegorical or layered; instead, it delivered the sort of mayhem you'd find in the silent pictures of an earlier age, complete with damsels in distress shrieking at approaching circular saws and heroes left hogtied on train tracks. In one strip, for example, Harry and Belinda are aboard a yacht when the dastardly Rudolph hops on the rudder and hijacks the boat. Harry turns the wheel just so, turning the boat into a spinning top and creating a whirlpool that empties the ocean. After tying Rudolph to the mast, he extends his arm to Belinda, and they traipse away to shore. Another strip sees Harry using his private plane and a crateful of rotten eggs to foil Rudolph's plot yet again. And unlike most other strips, *Hairbreadth Harry* didn't present a fresh adventure each week: instead, Kahles was one of the pioneers of strip serialization, creating multiweek arcs comprising installments that ended with cliff-hangers and drove Lee to the newsstand to see what happened next. That, to a lover of rhythm, was the perfect syncopation, a beat regularly interrupted by some titillating variation. It was this energy that moved him the most, and he soon sought to replicate it wherever he went.

Which, really, mostly meant high school. Lee attended

DeWitt Clinton High School, a castlelike structure overlooking twenty-one acres of playing fields in the Bronx. Several years earlier, two other Jewish boys, Will Eisner and Robert Kahn, had attended the same school; the first went on to create *The Spirit*, one of the most revered and influential comic strips ever conceived, and the second changed his name to Bob Kane and gave birth to Batman. Like them, Lee joined the staff of the *Magpie*, the school's literary magazine, but he wasn't interested in writing, editing, or drawing. The fun, he thought, was on the promotional end of things, selling the magazine to the readers. He appointed himself publicity director and made a name for himself sliding from one social circle to the next, talking up the magazine. Impressed with his gifts, his pals started calling him Gabby. "You always knew that he was going to be successful," one of them recalled years later. "It was a given."[6]

This vision of Lee as an irrepressible winner is one that Lee himself worked hard to cultivate. In his yearbook, he wrote, with characteristic gusto, that his goal was to "reach the top— and STAY there!" And if he couldn't reach the top just yet, he'd have to draw attention to himself in other ways. Some were outright goofy: one day, he walked in to the *Magpie*'s offices in the Tower, the high school's turret, only to find that a painter working there had gone on his lunch break and left behind his ladder. Impulsively, Lee climbed up and wrote his message on the ceiling: "Stan Lee is God." It was the first time the young Stanley Lieber publicly used the name that would make him famous, and his prank made a great impression on his friends.

He wasn't always so blunt or playful. One of his favorite stories, which he repeated throughout his life, involved his domination of the venerated *New York Herald Tribune* essay competition for high school students. Each week, the newspaper invited its young readers to argue, in 250 words or fewer, for what they believed was the most significant news story of the past seven days. Seven essays would then be chosen, and one writer among them crowned the winner and rewarded with fame as well as a $20 prize, or more than $350 in 2020 currency. Lee entered it when he was fifteen, and won first prize. He tried again the following week and again came out on top. He did the same thing on week three, by now having earned a small fortune and prompting an editor at the *Herald* to write and ask that he please stop writing and give other kids a chance.

It's a sweet anecdote. It is also, most likely, completely false: diving into the *Herald*'s archives, two scholars working on a biography of Lee found no first prize awarded to a Stanley Martin Lieber, only a single seventh-place finish on May 21, 1938. He received an honorable mention a week later, and, after that, nothing.[7]

To look at Lee's embellishment as a lie, or to merely excuse it as a figment of an anxious teen's insecurities, is to miss the point. Lee had it just right: the anecdote is worth retelling because, like one of the origin stories he was later so adept at creating for his heroes, it shows him, an ordinary kid, discovering his superpower. Just what that power was is harder to define; it's neither writing, really, nor self-promotion. Instead, it's the gift of plugging in to what filmmaker Werner Herzog called "the ecstatic truth" that hums just below the surface of art and life alike, frequently escaping the ears of those attuned only to the thud of recorded facts.[8]

As Lee would learn decades later, there was hardly a better job description for a maker of myths, whose task was not merely to invent colorful new worlds but to look deep into our own and find there new meanings buried underneath the rocky terrain of inertia and conventional wisdom.

None of these insights, however, was yet accessible to the teenager who spent his spare time working odd jobs to bring in a few extra dollars. A stint as an errand boy for a trouser manufacturer left him exhausted; he was giddy when, a few weeks after his start, he was summoned to the boss's office and summarily fired. He was an usher at the Rivoli Theater on Broadway, a job he loved but soon lost as well. He delivered sandwiches to offices and wrote obituaries for famous people who were still alive, to be published by the news wires on the occasion of their eventual demise. When he thought about a career, he wished he could become the sort of lawyer who delivered thundering speeches in the courtroom, but that required going to law school, and Lee had neither the time nor the money for that. Seventeen and underemployed, he asked Robbie Solomon, his uncle, for advice.

Solomon shrugged his shoulders. He himself was working for a company called Timely Publications, a magazine publisher owned by another relative, one Martin Goodman. Maybe, Solomon told his nephew, they'll have an opening for a young man who likes to write. An interview was arranged, and Lee, wearing his best outfit, arrived at the imposing McGraw-Hill building in midtown Manhattan. The emerald-and-blue-tinged Beaux Arts skyscraper made him nervous; years later he'd write in an unpublished memoir that the building "seemed to be made entirely of glass."[9] He took the elevator to Timely's offices, told the secretary his name, and waited for his uncle to come and get him. When Solomon emerged and escorted his nephew inside, Lee had his first glimpse at the house that Martin Goodman had built.

The ninth of thirteen siblings, Goodman was born in Brooklyn in 1908, to impoverished Jews who had emigrated from Russia. His father, a construction worker, fell from a rooftop and broke his back, leaving him unable to work and causing the family, forever behind on the rent, to dodge from one shabby apartment to the next. In the fifth grade, Goodman was forced to drop out of school and work menial jobs to help support the family. He hated each occupation more passionately than the previous one and eventually hopped a train and escaped into the life of a hobo, recording his impressions in his journals.

When he eventually returned to New York, he began working in the magazine industry, but his employer soon folded. Feeling as if he had nothing to lose, Goodman convinced a partner that they should start a publishing company of their own.

Not a particularly discerning reader—"fans," he told an interviewer once, "are not interested in quality"[10]—Goodman published schlock, from Lone Ranger knockoffs to thinly veiled retellings of popular detective stories, selling each issue for fifteen cents. He reserved refinement not for his art but for his person, dressing in elegant pink shirts, wire-rim glasses, and a bow tie, a distinguished appearance made even more striking by his prematurely white hair. As his empire expanded to include smash hits like *Two Gun Western* and *Sex Health*, he made sure his relatives all had jobs, hiring several of his brothers and making them all call him Mr. Goodman. He was quick to copy other people's successes, just as quick to cancel a title he felt wasn't working well, and forever mindful of his own comforts. Each day, after lunch, he'd retire to his office, lie on his chaise lounge, stare at the sign that hung on the wall that read "Don't forget to relax," and take a long, restorative nap. The writers and artists working for him for a few dollars a page had no such privilege.

Three of them were crowded into an eighteen-by-ten room when Lee was ushered in by Solomon, and none got up to greet the friendly teenager. Lee was struck by how comically different they were from one another, like a silent film trio: Joe Simon was tall and thin and spoke in a booming, confident voice; his pal Jack Kirby was short and irritable; and a third, Syd Shores, was an art school graduate accustomed to keeping quiet after nearly a decade spent making a living distilling whiskey. Solomon pointed to Lee. "This is my nephew," he said. "Can you find something for him to do?"[11] Accustomed to Goodman's cheerful nepotism, the three didn't even bother pretending to interview Lee; he was hired on the spot, for eight dollars a week, as the new errand boy for Timely Comics.

It was a brand-new division of Goodman's company, and Simon, Kirby, and Shores were its first and only employees. Even in a company dedicated to publishing lowbrow titles, comic books were still considered the bottom of the barrel; its creators sometimes bitterly joked that their peers regarded them as just one rung beneath pornographers. But Goodman made his fortune by closely reading the market, and the market was telling him that comic books were becoming big business.

Which was surprising to anyone who had paid any attention to the industry's strange inception. For decades, comic strips had been published exclusively in newspapers; collecting them in dedicated volumes made as much sense as reprinting a collection of the month's sporting news, say, or reports of last year's weather. But in 1933, a salesman for Eastern Color Printing had the idea to put out eight pages' worth of old comic strips on newsprint sheets and give them away as a promotional gimmick. His name was Maxwell Charles Gaines, a man condemned to restless innovation by his very body: when he was four, he leaned out of a second-story window and fell to the ground, his leg catching on a picket fence and leaving him with a chronic injury. Constantly in pain, he was impatient and short-tempered. He worked as a teacher, a principal, a haberdasher, and an assembly line cog in a factory making munitions, but he felt that all these positions were beneath him. He was fond of get-rich-quick schemes—he once tried to market an anti-Prohibition tie emblazoned with the slogan "We Want Beer!"—but all failed.

He changed his name from Max Ginzberg to the more gentilic moniker by which he'd eventually become known, and found his way to the printing industry, working on commission. Eastern Color, he soon observed, printed its orders in three shifts, but the third shift, beginning in the dead of night, was slower than the rest, which meant that the machines often stood idle. Gaines rushed to Harry Wildernberg, his manager, and proposed that they use the time instead to print something that a large client, maybe Procter & Gamble, might want to give away to its customers as a special promotion. Comic strips, abundant and popular, were an obvious choice. Gaines selected a few and printed them, side by side, on tabloid pages he then folded in half and stapled together.

It was a massive success, and later that year, Gaines put out another volume, this time lining up a few sponsors, including Wheatena, Canada Dry, and Phillips' Dental Magnesia.[12] He wondered, however, whether readers would pay for his comic reprints, and the following February he decided to run a little test by publishing another volume and selling copies for ten cents apiece. He called it *Famous Funnies*.

Nervous, Eastern Color Printing refused to ship the magazine to newsstands, choosing to minimize the risk of embarrassment by selling it in department stores instead. The company printed thirty-five thousand copies; they sold out almost immediately. A second iteration soon followed, this time distributed widely; it lost money. But by issue number seven, *Famous Funnies* brought in a bundle, and the series remained profitable and grew in popularity.[13] Imitators soon followed: by 1941, thirty comic book publishers were producing more than 150 titles per month, with combined sales of more than fifteen million copies reaching more than sixty million Americans.[14]

But not all of these fledgling publishers could afford paying royalties for popular strips like *Mutt and Jeff* or *Hairbreadth Harry*. Many chose instead to hire young artists to write and illustrate original stories.

Or maybe "artists" wasn't the right word. "It was wide open," Joe Kubert, one of the industry's earliest and most successful illustrators, recalled. "Nobody knew what they were doing. If you wanted to do comics and you had a little bit of talent—hell, even if you didn't have any talent—there was work for you. Maybe you had a lot of talent but you had a different kind of style, something unique and different, that the art directors in the slick magazines didn't like. You could be a genius, you could be a nobody, a little kid from Brooklyn like me, or some kind of nut. The doors were open to any and all."[15]

Those who walked through them, however, were mainly young Jews, in large part because they found most other doors locked. "We couldn't get into newspaper strips or advertising," Al Jaffee, who would later find fame with *MAD* magazine, recalled. "Ad agencies wouldn't hire a Jew. One of the reasons we Jews drifted into the comic-book business is that most of the comic-book publishers were Jewish. So there was no discrimination there."[16] Besides, just as they had done with the movies, Jews—many of them first-generation Americans—saw comic books as a chance to weave themselves into the national narrative, to tell stories that were both explicitly Jewish and profoundly American and that, by means of some mystical alchemy, melded the two cultures into one.

Not surprisingly, the stories they told drew heavily from their insecurities. Some of these anxieties were collective, the tremors of a minority in a nation where millions tuned in weekly to the antisemitic rants of Father Coughlin or found inspiration in Henry Ford's *The International Jew*. But others were darkly personal. In Cleveland, in the summer of 1932, a young boy named Jerry Siegel was at home on Kimberly Avenue, a quiet tree-lined street populated by upwardly mobile Jews and dotted with institutions that catered to their tastes, from Solomon's Delicatessen to Spector's Creamery. Someone knocked on the door and delivered the news: Jerry's father, Mitchell, had been closing up his clothing store when an armed robber walked in. A few minutes later, a neighboring shopkeeper, noticing the open door, walked into the store to check on Mitchell. He found him lying in a pool of blood, with two bullet holes in his chest. Devastated, Jerry's mother kept a tight watch on her son, who found solace in comic strips. Together with his high school friend, Joe Shuster, he began working on a hero of their own, a man who would be strong enough to ward off any danger and gallant enough to leap to the help of those who needed it. They called him Superman, and in the first cartoon they ever drew of him, he proved his might by stopping an armed robbery.

Shuster and Siegel tried their best to sell their hero to a publisher, but none would buy. Will Eisner, now the head of his own thriving comics syndication company, told the boys their caped hero wasn't the sort of thing likely to amuse his readers. "I told them they weren't ready for prime time," he recalled in an interview decades later. "So much for my sound editorial judgment!"[17] But the two Clevelanders refused to give up, and, after years of sending around their samples, they finally caught the eye of Max Gaines.

Fired from Eastern Color Printing—Gaines's foul temper must have overshadowed even his vision and his success—he was now back to hustling, and a teenaged cartoonist, Sheldon Mayer, told him he'd seen some strips floating around that featured a neat hero who couldn't be beat. Gaines had Lieber and Shuster piece together a few of their drafts and took it to his friends Harry Donenfeld and Jack Liebowitz, who had just taken over a publishing company called National Periodicals. Trusting Gaines's intuition, they paid the two young creators $130 for all future rights to Superman.

The new hero made his debut in 1938, in a new magazine called *Action Comics*. By the nineteenth issue, it was selling 500,000 copies per month, four times as many as the next-most successful title. Soon, Superman was awarded his own comic book series, the first superhero to earn that distinction. By the time Stan Lee walked into Timely Comics, Superman comics were selling more than 1,250,000 copies per month, in addition to appearing in strips in newspapers in more than three hundred cities.[18]

The Man of Steel, then, was the one to beat for anyone working in comics in 1939. And as Lee soon learned, Jack Kirby and Joe Simon had an idea for a hero they believed would give Superman a good fight at the newsstands. In fact, they had already sent the first issue to the printer. Its cover featured their newest hero, Captain America, smashing Adolf Hitler in the face.

3

Getting in the Way

As TIMELY COMICS' new errand boy, Stan Lee had little to do. Once or twice a day, he'd run down and get Joe Simon something to eat, or empty Jack Kirby's wastebasket, or run pages around to the production department. But the rest of the time he was just milling about, not something that came naturally to the outgoing Gabby. To pass the time and keep his spirits high, he carried a small ocarina and played it from time to time, driving Kirby to distraction. The artist was amazed that the new kid would have the gall to walk around making merry tunes—occasionally he'd even open the door to Martin Goodman's office and blow a couple of squeaky notes his way—but also grateful for Lee's good cheer and enthusiasm. No request, no matter how menial, was beneath the teenager. On the contrary: he was eager to please, constantly asking Kirby whether his inkwell needed filling. Lee's attitude, Kirby and Simon decided, was more endearing than annoying.

When he wasn't doing his best to curry favor, Lee was figuring out his new industry. It wasn't an easy task. Never a fanatical comic strip reader, he wasn't immersed, like some of his contemporaries, in the intricacies of the genre and its creators. And Timely itself, he soon learned, was a complicated operation, a testament to its owner's seismic sensibilities.

Sensing that comics was becoming a big business, Lee learned that Goodman had contracted Lloyd Jacquet, a pipe-smoking former colonel who ran a company called Funnies, Inc., to create titles for Timely to sell. Jacquet, in turn, farmed out the work to two twenty-one-year-olds who worked out of a Manhattan bar called the Webster. They created two characters, both of which were soon smash hits: the Human Torch and the Sub-Mariner. The first was a demonic creature created in a lab by a mad scientist and intent on literally setting the world on fire. The second was the alter ego of Prince Namor, heir to a magical underwater kingdom destroyed by nuclear testing. Namor, too, was hell-bent on revenge, although, unlike his fiery friend, his rage was often quelled when he noticed a particularly fetching earth maiden.

Reading through these offerings, Lee noticed a few things he liked. First, Jacquet's artists, Carl Burgos and Bill Everett, didn't bother erecting fictitious cities for their heroes to defend or destroy. Why set up the action in Metropolis, say, when all you had to do was step out of your speakeasy and there, in all its glory, was New York? The Sub-Mariner, then, took great pleasure in destroying Manhattan's finest landmarks, from the George Washington Bridge to the Holland Tunnel. Making things even more realistic, Burgos and Everett had their creations visit each other's volumes, which gave readers the sense that they inhabited the same expansive fictional universe.

But Lee didn't get to work with the two enterprising creators. Reluctant to rely on Jacquet for much longer—Goodman preferred not to be in business with anyone not directly in his employ and under his command—and aware that no one in comics was particularly loyal to any one publisher, Goodman decided that if he was going to make a mark in the industry, he needed to make sure all his titles were created in-house. He hired Simon and Kirby, who in turn hired Syd Shores. And they hoped for a hit with Captain America.

Like his creators, Simon and Kirby, Cap, as the square-jawed hero was soon known, was obsessed with the Nazis. He was born Steve Rogers, a scrawny kid from the Lower East Side who desperately wanted to prove himself an American hero—not unlike Kirby himself, who was born Jacob Kurtzberg but changed his name to make it sound more like Jimmy Cagney's. Turned away at the recruitment office for being too skinny and unfit, Rogers volunteers for a top-secret mission and is injected with a serum developed by the subtly named Dr. Josef Reinstein. Immediately, his muscles bulk, his shoulders broaden, his back firms up. "We shall call you Captain America, son," an emotional Dr. Reinstein says while ogling his creation, "because like you, America shall gain the strength and the will to safeguard our shores!"[1]

The writing was nothing if not sincere. Kirby and Simon were both the children of impoverished Jewish immigrants—Simon's father came from Leeds, Kirby's parents from Austria—and the two, following the darkening news from Europe with growing anxiety, were appalled to learn how many Americans advocated for isolationism.

They weren't alone: On May 26, 1940, as Kirby and Simon were at work on their newest creation, President Roosevelt gave a fireside chat that captured precisely what the two were thinking. "There are many among us who closed their eyes," he said, "from lack of interest or lack of knowledge; honestly and sincerely thinking that the many hundreds of miles of salt water made the American Hemisphere so remote that the people of North and Central and South America could go on living in the midst of their vast resources without reference to, or danger from, other Continents of the world." Roosevelt then went on to describe the robust state of the nation's armaments, before ending with a promise that America would not turn a blind eye to Hitler's brutalities. "It is the task of our generation, yours and mine," he concluded. "We defend the foundations laid down by your fathers. We build a life for generations yet unborn. We defend and we build a way of life, not for America alone, but for all mankind. Ours is a high duty, a noble task."[2]

Kirby and Simon listened intently. "The opponents of the war were all quite well organized," Simon told an interviewer decades later. "We wanted to have our say too."[3]

They gave their creation a red, white, and blue outfit, and a name that left no doubt as to his purpose: he was a paragon of American military intervention. And lest anyone still believe that the perfidious Nazis were confined to their European haunts, Kirby and Simon packed the first issue with intrigue galore. No sooner does Rogers complete his transformation than a Nazi spy shouts "Death to the dogs of democracy!" and shoots Dr. Reinstein, killing him and shattering the serum that might've created scores more superheroes.

Rogers eliminates the brute, but his life hardly gets easier. Nazi spies and saboteurs are all around him, threatening not only Jews in faraway countries but innocent Americans at home. The comic lays it on thick, but just in case anyone missed out on the message, Kirby and Simon attached a little clip-out form, inviting young readers to send in ten cents and become members of Captain America's Sentinels of Liberty, helping Cap in his "war against the spies and enemies in our midst who threaten our very independence." Many kids answered the call; many more grown-ups found the new comic book's language appalling in its unabashed support for the still not entirely popular war. But the Captain was an instant success, and Lee, not content to fill inkwells for long, wanted in on the action. He got his break right away.

To qualify for reduced Second Class Mail rates, a comic book had to contain enough printed words per issue to qualify as a magazine. That meant that someone had to write a two-page long story, a task both Kirby and Simon considered a waste of their time. Lee, on the other hand, was eager to take a stab. With the third issue of *Captain America*, he got his chance.

Titled "Captain America Foils the Traitor's Revenge," it's far from the sparkling stuff Lee would deliver in his prime. But anyone interested in a portrait of the artist as a young man will not be disappointed. The action begins in medias res, with Colonel Stevens chastising a soldier named Haines. "There is no place in this army camp for the likes of you," the colonel barks. "You have lied, cheated, spied, and stolen."[4] Although we're not told explicitly in whose service said Haines might be, it is obvious, given the comic's context, that he is another one of the infinitude of Nazis lurking in every corner of American life. Steve Rogers, standing nearby, listens intently; he hears the retreating Haines ominously threatening to return with a vengeance, a narrative flourish that will soon become a Lee staple. Later that night, as Rogers and his teenaged sidekick Bucky are horsing around in their tent, they hear Haines approaching with two henchmen, headed straight for the colonel's tent. Rogers swiftly puts on his Captain America uniform and rushes to the colonel's defense, overpowering the villains with ease. The next morning, Colonel Stevens, unaware of Steve Rogers's secret identity, chides the soldier for not rushing to Captain America's aid. "Oh why can't I have some soldiers like Captain America in this army—instead of YOU!" the colonel laments as Rogers smiles knowingly and walks away.

It's doubtful that anyone at the time was paying much attention to dialogue—the comic book's readers were mostly kids who cheered on the Captain's fists, not his flair with words—

but those who were could have easily spotted a difference between Lee's Cap and the square-jawed he-man created by Kirby and Simon. Theirs was humorless, and his language recalled the colloquial, intentionally misspelled dialects of so many early comic strip stars. The comic book Cap appeared on the scene, swung his arms, and said things like "So you're one of the Phewrer's flunkies," or "If you enjoy life at all, you'll start talking, fast!" Lee's Captain, on the other hand, was something closer to a real human being: we see him relaxing in his tent, playing checkers and trading good-natured insults with Bucky. "You don't know how tired it makes me to beat you all the time," he quips, and when, a few lines later, it's time for Rogers to leap into costume and into action, it's not an abstraction we see punching and grabbing but a more layered character we've come to know and love. Instinctively, from that very first story, Lee wanted readers to care as much about Steve Rogers as they did about Captain America. And that, in the comic book scene of the time, was nothing short of a transcendental insight.

Consider, for a moment, Lee's competition. Anyone writing comic books in 1941 was toiling in the shadow of two colossal figures, Superman and Batman. And neither figure was, in any discernible sense, recognizably human. Following the adventures of the Man of Steel or the Caped Crusader, one quickly understood that these two totemic figures were not much more than the sum of their derring-do. That's because they were, really, not much more than the embodiment of the two warring poles of American spiritual life. Batman was modernism personified, a wealthy and privileged Brahmin with no special powers who used his endless resources and superior intelligence to deliver a vastly improved version of local government, one unencumbered by all that pesky business of accountability and transparency. Jim Gordon, Gotham City's commissioner of police, saw Batman much as FDR's critics regarded the president during the New Deal, resentful of this figure of authority who swept in with little regard for tradition and altered reality by the force of his will, but powerless to do anything but collaborate with the iron-willed patrician. Superman, on the other hand, can easily be read as a creature of the fundamentalist imagination. He might've had a vaguely Hebrew name—Kal-El, meaning either "voice of God" or "the entirety of God"—and he might have been, like Moses, discovered in a small basket as a baby and raised in a foreign land, but he bears a greater resemblance to Christ, a luminous figure descendent from the heavens to redeem mankind by virtue of his grace. In each issue, he fights corrupt politicians, crooked businessmen, and anyone else in a position of power who tries to lord it over the meek. Also in every issue, he takes a bullet—or a train, or a car—for our sins, and in each case rises again to inspire us with his vision of heavenly love. All we have to do is believe in him. It's no coincidence, then, that when Warner Bros. released the 2006 dud *Superman Returns*, it directed much of the publicity efforts at the evangelical community, marketing the movie as a Christian parable for the ages.

Distilled to two pure manifestations and presented in comic book form, the tension between the fundamentalists and the modernists played out in an even more stilted fashion than it did elsewhere in American public life. It was one thing for men like Clarence Darrow and William Jennings Bryan, two patricians with deep American roots, to duke it out among themselves; but when the same Protestant tremors that have always troubled America's religious imagination were picked up and mimicked by immigrant Jews, the result was simultaneously epic and strained. The heroes these Jewish artists created, Superman and Batman, could never step outside the bounds of their self-contained ideals. They were, Lee observed on several occasions, perpetual motion machines that had only one, simple setting: swoop down, save day, retreat, repeat. If you were an attuned reader, and Lee was nothing if not that, you would soon see that this monolithic approach to mythmaking wasn't just tedious—why, after all, bother reading the next volume when you already know with some precision how the plot might unfold?—but also morally dubious. Superman, a Christ without Christianity, is a deus ex machina; he exists outside of the realm of human comprehension, and his relationship with us mortals, as far as we can understand, is governed by nothing but dumb luck.

One of the most remarkable retellings of the Superman story, *Red Son*, plays on this idea precisely. As a child, the Scottish comic book creator Mark Millar was observing the Cold War and wondering what might have happened if the Man of Steel happened to fight for the Commies instead. In 2003, he published a three-issue masterpiece that examines this very premise: Superman's father, Jor-El, lingers for a moment longer before dispatching his son toward Earth, and the planet's revolution means that the baby's spacecraft now lands not in the cornfields of Kansas but in the potato fields of a collective farm in the Ukraine. He soon becomes a favorite of Stalin's, and instead of standing up for "truth, justice, and the American way," he grows into "a champion of the common worker who fights a never-ending battle for Stalin, socialism, and the international expansion of the Warsaw Pact."[5]

The Soviet Superman soon meets Batman, whose parents, in this retelling, were murdered not by a thug in a dark alley but by the NKVD, and the two do battle, propelling an increasingly complicated plot forward. By the end, the supers all perish, leaving Lex Luthor—traditionally Superman's archenemy—to govern as the benevolent head of a world government that has rid itself of its dependency on anything and anyone, like the Man of Steel, that isn't thoroughly human. Beyond the fun of entertaining radically divergent versions of well-known stories, the comic book is jarring because it rekindles our deepest theological anxieties concerning our relationship with an almighty supreme being we can neither see nor know.

Captain America was nothing like that. Genetically altered as he might have been, he was still thoroughly human, as were his preoccupations. It wasn't a strange element from space, Kryptonite, that could bring him down, but a much more earthly danger, Nazism. By the second issue, he was darting off to a concentration camp in the Black Forest to save an American financier kidnapped by the Germans, all the while delivering zingers like "Heel Hitler" or "Now come out of your hole, Ratzis!"[6]

How influential was his creators' Judaism in determining the Captain's predilections? Asked that question frequently about several of his heroes, Lee was always coy. "You know, I have no idea," he told a radio interviewer. "I never really thought of it. It is strange when you mention it that the best-known characters were done by Jewish writers. I guess that is an odd thought."[7] But beyond the obvious notion that first generation Jewish immigrants who still had relatives in Europe would be upset by Hitler's rise, a closer look at Captain America himself suggests a deeply Jewish sensibility coming to the fore, a sensibility rarely before seen in comics.

Unlike Bruce Wayne, Batman's alter ego, Steve Rogers wasn't a glamorous billionaire. In fact, whenever he appeared early in the series, it was usually in the midst of some menial task, and superiors often threatened him with some sort of demotion. Also unlike Wayne, his motivations weren't personal; there were no traumas in his past, and no reason for him to become the Captain other than a desire to do his duty to his country. As a result, his relationship with the army remained much more cordial than Batman's with the police; the Captain couldn't begin to imagine himself as something other than an instrument in service of a larger cause, a communal worldview that was at odds with Batman's solipsistic one. Put crudely, his greatest desire is to assimilate and become the epitome of American manhood, a task he can achieve, ironically, only by hiding his true identity as a creature endowed with very special powers. But unlike Batman and Superman, he isn't lonely, because, unlike them, he is powered not by Protestant ideals but by a radically different theological concept, a profoundly Jewish one.

Discussing what the coming of the Messiah—the final redeemer, the ultimate superhero—might look like, the wise rabbis of the Talmud described a vision the Captain might have endorsed. "The only difference between this world and the messianic era," they wrote, "is subjugation of the exiles to other kingdoms, from which the Jewish people will be released. However, in other respects, the world will remain as it is, as it is written: 'Because the poor will not cease from within the land' (Deuteronomy 15:11). Society will not change, and wars will continue to be waged."[8] In this radical vision, no savior, caped or otherwise, appears to put an end to history. Instead, we're promised only the removal of subjugation—which is to say, we're promised more freedom—before being reminded that we would then need to put that freedom to use in addressing the eternal problems of humanity.

Michael Walzer helpfully summed up this idea by writing that God will not "send the Messiah until the people are ready to receive him. But when they are ready, it might be said, they won't need a messiah."[9] In other words, Jewish eschatology does not wait for a divine creature to descend from the heavens or from Krypton and fix all that is broken. It reminds us that if we work hard and support one another here on Earth, we'll soon be free, which, really, is all we could ever hope for. The Captain, with his strong arms and stronger commitment to helping all those around him, is not a terrible prototype of the Jewish messianic idea.

Writing lines for the Captain, then, was a perfect task for someone like Lee, always on the hunt for a story that revealed some deeper and nonliteral truth about human existence. He was now free to treat Steve Rogers as he had once treated Stanley Lieber, carefully constructing a narrative that was both believable and exciting and that spoke not to what was apparent but to what was possible. That no one was reading his work didn't matter to him one bit. "It gave me a feeling of grandeur," he later told an interviewer, and his enthusiasm soon impressed his bosses, who were swamped with work and only too happy to let the kid milling about the office pick up some of the slack.[10]

A few months later, in August 1941, writing in *Captain America* number 5, Lee had his debut in comic form with a story called "Headline Hunter, Foreign Correspondent"; it was well written and zippy, but Lee's big break didn't come until later that month, when he was given the chance to write the first superhero of his own creation for a new title Timely was putting out called *U.S.A. Comics*. The hero's name was Jack Frost.

It's not hard to guess where Lee found his inspiration. With fire and water already spoken for with the Human Torch and the Sub-Mariner, Lee, searching the elements, must've stumbled upon ice, and the name Jack Frost added a dimension of familiarity. In Lee's telling, he is a mysterious and powerful figure, part man and part icicle, residing at the North Pole. Hitting the stride that would soon become his trademark, Lee introduced his new hero with bated breath: "The Far North! Challenging! Mysterious! Foreboding! The land that no man really knows . . . In this great, frozen waste, surrounded by an eternal, deathly quiet, lives a person we have all heard of but few men have seen—the King of the Cold—Jack Frost!"[11]

The language—just on the right side of flowery, stylishly crafted yet accessible, excited and still economical—was Lee's way into the story. No sooner do we meet Frost slouching on his ice shelf than a dying explorer named Dr. Forbes appears, begging the cool hero to travel to New York and rescue his daughter from the treacherous, murderous Mike Zelby. Driven by a sense of justice, Frost obeys, but his reception in the Big Apple is chilly. He reports to the police, but the officers he meets mock him, sending him into a rage of flying icicles and

cold fronts. He decides to rescue Dr. Forbes's daughter by himself, which leads to more feats of frozen strength. Bested and
furious, Zelby sets the room on fire as Frost and Ms. Forbes are
fleeing, but the hero freezes their path to safety.

The young woman begs him to go back and save Zelby
from the burning building; "You can rescue Zelby," she says,
"you must! Only the law has the right to punish him!" Frost
contemplates it, but ultimately refuses, saying that Zelby must
pay for his crimes. "If you refuse to save a man when you're
able to," a troubled Ms. Forbes says, invoking the Talmudic
principle that saving one soul is akin to saving the world entire,
"that makes you practically a murderer!" The police agree: arriving just in time to watch Zelby burn to death, they accuse
Frost of murdering the villain, and move in to arrest him.
Hurt and livid, Jack Frost vanishes, leaving the reader to guess
whether he'll ever return and, more important, whether he'll
remain a hero or, embittered, turn bad.

Just six pages long, the story introduces the twin pillars of
Lee's storytelling sensibility. The first holds that a hero is interesting only if he exists in the shadowy space between two clashing ideals, struggling to determine what's right and, doing so,
sacrificing his own immaculate goodness. The second insists
that the engine that moves the story forward be morality, not
plot. Years later, Lee's most celebrated creation, Spider-Man,
would face a conundrum similar to Jack Frost's: he refuses to
foil a burglary—that, he argues, is a job for the police—only to
learn later that the same burglar has gone on to murder his beloved uncle Ben. The guilt and hurt that ensue propel him to
take up a life of crime fighting, and he remains haunted by the
specter of his own moral failure. For a nineteen-year-old first
timer, the issues confronted in the Jack Frost debut were tre-
mendous, and deeply promising, insights.

Kirby and Simon must have agreed, as Lee was given free
rein to come up with another hero, Destroyer, a reporter who

is injected with a powerful serum and becomes a mighty menace to Nazis everywhere. He was a lot like Captain America, but few readers cared—comic books were growing exponentially, and readers wanted more titles and fast. By 1941, comic books were selling seven to ten million copies per month, generating between eight and twelve million dollars in revenue annually. Traditional children's books, by comparison, brought in just two million dollars that year.[12]

But meteoric growth didn't translate into stability, and comic book publishers were increasingly busy trying to poach each other's talent. Soon, Lee began noticing that Kirby and Simon were taking ever-longer lunch breaks, and appeared to be huddling and whispering more than usual. One day, as the two were rushing out of the office again, he confronted them. "You guys must be working on something of your own!" he said.[13]

Reluctantly, Kirby and Simon told Lee their secret. They were never too happy, they said, with the idea that they'd created one of the most successful characters in comics history only to receive modest compensation and hold none of the rights to their work. Entrepreneurial, they had negotiated an agreement with Martin Goodman that paid them royalties, and they were happy to make a bit of extra cash working clandestinely as freelancers for Timely's competitors. But a few months earlier, they said, one of Goodman's assistants revealed to them that the boss was deducting almost all of the company's overhead from *Captain America*'s profits. Enraged, the two decided to jump ship, and called Jack Liebowitz at the company now known as DC Comics, the industry's leader, home of Superman and Batman. Overjoyed, Liebowitz promised each artist a retainer of five hundred dollars per week, and instructed them to come up with new ideas for comic books posthaste. They had rented a cheap hotel room not far from Timely's offices, where they were working on the new heroes they were about to present to DC.

Lee asked to join the two in their clandestine brainstorming sessions, and Kirby and Simon eventually agreed, even though they grumbled that the kid was "getting in the way."[14] A few days later, Kirby and Simon were summoned to a meeting with Martin Goodman's brothers.

"You guys are working for DC," Abe Goodman hissed at them. "You haven't been true to us. You haven't been loyal to us. You should be ashamed of yourself." Once they were done with the latest issue of *Captain America*, Abe continued, they should take their possessions and leave for good. At this particular meeting, Simon noted, Stan Lee "was nowhere to be seen."[15]

When asked about the affair, as he was frequently later in life, Lee delivered a very different account, swearing that not only had he not ratted out Kirby and Simon, but that the two were not even fired. They left unexpectedly, he said; "Truth is, I never knew exactly why they left."[16] But Kirby remained convinced that Lee was the culprit. "He never gave up on that idea," Simon remembered decades later, "and hated [Lee] for the rest of his life—to the day he died."[17] Kirby himself was just as vocal about his distaste for Lee. "The next time I see that little son of a bitch," he said to Simon shortly after they were fired, "I'm going to kill him."[18]

With his star artists gone and business booming, Martin Goodman had a problem: he needed an editor who knew the business well enough, and he needed him right away. Looking around the office, the only person he saw was Lee, a smiling teenager with an ocarina who was also a budding writer with a winning attitude. Following his gut, Goodman appointed Lee to be the editor of Timely Comics. It was the sort of stunning ascent Lee had previously fabricated to impress his friends; but now that it was real, he received a pat on the back, a small raise, and a company to run.

4

Playwright

THE BEST WAY TO RUN Timely Comics, Stan Lee quickly realized, was to act as if Jack Kirby and Joe Simon had never left. Rather than try to assert himself or chart out a new artistic course, Lee clung to every tried-and-true title he'd inherited from his predecessors, keeping production as tight as it had been when the cocreators of Captain America were still running the show. But Kirby and Simon were industry veterans who had been writing and drawing comics since childhood, and Lee, fast learner though he was, had much catching up to do.

To give himself solid ground to stand on in the meantime, he hired an army of freelancers, starting with Burgos and Everett, creators of the Sub-Mariner and the Human Torch, who had been summarily dismissed by Martin Goodman less than two years earlier. Still, freelancers could do only so much; a publishing house needed, at the very least, an editor in chief, an art director, and a head writer. All three duties now fell to Lee, who was working increasingly longer days to meet his obligations. Drawing on his experience as the marketing director of his high school paper, he was eager to make Timely seem like a much larger and more consequential shop, which was easily achieved by making up a host of pen names: Some of the stories were credited to Stan Lee, some to Stan Martin, some to Neel Nats.

Three junior assistants helped him keep track of all these alter egos, but, as artists who had worked with him in those days later recalled, Lee didn't seem as if he needed any real assistance. Anyone walking down Timely's halls could hear him on the phone with this artist or the other, describing, with great enthusiasm and verve, entire plotlines he was making up as he went along. The stories were never groundbreaking, but they weren't any worse than anything anyone else was putting out, and that a teenager with little experience could invent them out of whole cloth with such eloquence and at such speed struck Lee's colleagues and employees as uncanny.

Aware of his boy wonder status, Lee played up his persona as much as he could. Sometimes, he'd come to the office wearing a four-color beanie with a propeller on top, as if he were just an impish schoolboy who had somehow tricked the adults into trusting him. Often, he'd make colleagues sit and listen to an ocarina solo before talking business. Always, he'd deliver a new idea by standing up and acting out the plot, doing a different voice for each character and clapping his hands for emphasis during the big action scenes. More than one young and impressionable coworker compared him to Orson Welles. Always one to encourage hero worship of every sort, Lee made up yet another name for himself: Mr. Timely Comics.

Impressed, Martin Goodman gave Lee more rope. The boss was still intimately involved in every decision, from choosing the covers to determining which new hero survived and which was scrapped, but he was happy to let Lee run things his way. As long as the young editor could write two or three stories a week and make sure no one missed a deadline, his job was secure.

And then came Pearl Harbor.

Almost immediately after Japan attacked the United States, nearly everyone Lee had ever worked with was in uniform. Joe Simon joined the Mounted Beach Patrol before being shipped off to basic training in Maryland. Jack Kirby was now private first class, Fifth Division, Third Army. Carl Burgos volunteered for the air force, and Bill Everett was in Officer Candidate School in Fort Belvoir, Virginia.

Lee could hardly stay put. "I think I could have gotten a deferment," he told an interviewer decades later, but "it was the kind of war you were a son of a bitch if you didn't get into it. It was too important not to fight."[1] Eager to get to the war's front line—he imagined he'd be in Europe by year's end—Lee called Vince Fago, a freelancer who was best known for working on Betty Boop and Popeye, as well as a host of adorable animal heroes like Ziggy Pig, Silly Seal, and Posty the Pelican Postman. "How'd you like my job?" he asked him, and Fago gladly accepted.[2] On November 9, 1942, seven weeks shy of his twentieth birthday, Stan Lee enlisted in the army.

Having aced his Army General Classification Test, and proving himself to be an intelligent and verbally adept recruit, Lee was assigned to the Signal Corps and sent to Fort Monmouth, New Jersey, for basic training. There he learned how to string and repair communications lines, which led the ever imaginative Lee to envision a future straight out of a *Captain America* comic, with himself sneaking into enemy territory and defying the Nazis by setting up crucial infrastructure. He felt another twinge of affinity for Steve Rogers when assigned to the same menial tasks that usually befell the hero in his unmasked moments, patrolling the perimeter in the freezing wind and watching out for German U-Boats. But neither the cold nor the strange new routine could dampen Lee's spirit of self-promotion, and he was soon busy telling anyone who would listen, his superiors first and foremost, that he was, despite his young age, a big shot writer and editor back in Manhattan.

Unbeknownst to him, writing and editing were high on the Signal Corps' priorities at the time. The nation was now mobilized into war, which meant that men of all walks of life and levels of education had joined the army and were expected to fight as one. These men needed to be trained, and long and cumbersome manuals proved less than ideal for those GIs whose reading comprehension left a lot to be desired. Films, the army quickly realized, were a much more effective medium: a training film took only a few minutes to watch and left little room for varying interpretations or misunderstandings. In a studio in Astoria, Queens, the Corps had built the largest sound stage in the Northeast and was now recruiting men under a special military designation: "Playwright."

Frank Capra, naturally, was one of them, as was Charles Addams, the *New Yorker* cartoonist and creator of the popular *Addams Family* strip. Theodor Geisel, soon and forever to be known as Dr. Seuss, was present, as was William Saroyan, who had won and rejected the Pulitzer Prize a few years earlier for his play *The Time of Your Life*. The desk right next to Saroyan's was Lee's.

He had little opportunity, however, to get to know his new famous brothers in arms. Much of his time was spent on TDY, or temporary duty, going from base to base and helping create whatever instructional materials they needed. Comic books, geared toward young children, provided a natural medium for exploring subject matter that was otherwise too complicated or too dull. When the Army Finance Department, for example, asked Lee to create a manual that would teach payroll officers how to disburse funds on time, he created a comic book starring a new hero, Fiscal Freddy, who humorously taught the bureaucrats how to work better and faster. "We were able to shorten the training period of payroll officers by more than 50 percent," Lee later said with characteristic aplomb. "I think I won the war single-handedly."[3] His biggest turn at glory, however, came when the army, treating tens of thousands of soldiers each month for sexually transmitted diseases, asked Lee to find some way of talking up safe sex. He came up with a poster featuring a smiling soldier and the caption "VD? Not me!" It became one of the army's ubiquitous bits of propaganda.

As effective and highly visible as his army work might have been, it left Lee with much time on his hands. Back at Timely, he was used to publishing five issues each week, a mad, headlong rush. His schedule as a soldier was far more relaxed, and so, hungry for a taste of his civilian life, he took on a host of freelance assignments from Vince Fago. The two set up a fool-proof system: Fago would put some assignment in the mail on Thursday, and Lee would receive it a day later and spend the weekend working. He'd mail it back on Monday, making Fago's Tuesday deadline. One Friday afternoon, however, Lee went to see the mail clerk, and was informed that no letter had arrived.

"Are you sure there's no letter for me?" he asked.

"Nah, nothin'," said the clerk.

Disappointed, Lee went on his way. The next day, however, he walked past the mail room and noticed that his cubbyhole indeed had a letter in it, with Timely's return address clearly visible. Annoyed, he marched to the clerk's office and demanded to be given his letter. That, the clerk replied, was impossible, as the mail room was shut until Monday morning. But waiting until Monday morning meant missing the deadline, a precedent Lee wasn't willing to set.

He picked up a screwdriver, marched back to the mail room, and unscrewed the hinge holding the padlock. After collecting his letter, he screwed it back on and spent the weekend working on his assignment for Timely, mailing it on Monday morning, on time as always. On Tuesday, however, he was ordered to report, on the double, to the office of one of the base's grumpier captains, who informed Lee that there was evidence to suggest he had burglarized the mail room and would now be placed in custody. Luckily for Lee, the base's commander knew him from his work on the Fiscal Freddy manual, and deemed him too valuable for prison.[4]

With the money he was making collecting salaries from both the army and Timely, Lee bought himself a jet-black, four-door Buick convertible with a red leather interior and whitewall tires. He spent much of his time and energy driving around and trying to impress women. He was always sore about having missed the college experience—"living on campus, having beer parties, getting laid every night"—and used his leisure in the army to make up for lost time. "I was in love a hundred times," he recalled years later. "They shipped me to different cities all over the country; every city I'd go to, I'd meet some other gal I thought was terrific."[5] But when the war finally ended, it was business, not romance, that was foremost on Lee's mind: as soon as he received his discharge papers, he jumped right into his Buick and motored to Manhattan, eager to resume his old post as Mr. Timely Comics.

But the industry Lee found on his return wasn't the same one he'd left behind just a few years earlier. The war having been won, readers seemed to have little appetite for brave men in tights running around fighting evil. But with so much of his professional identity embedded in coming up with new and exciting heroes, Lee refused to give up without a fight. If folks didn't care for a single superhero, he reasoned, maybe four or five or six would do the trick: in the fall of 1946, he launched a new title, *All Winners Comics*, banding together Captain America, the Human Torch, the Sub-Mariner, and a handful of other mildly popular characters, each complete with his or her own teenage sidekick. Intent on generating as much wattage as he could, Lee stuck a blurb on the cover that promised readers "a complete SIZZLING, ACTION THRILLER!"[6] To make sure that the story was strong, Lee hired Bill Finger, Batman's cocreator, to write a story about a mad villain attempting to steal a nuclear weapon. Nothing helped. The All Winners won no hearts and were unceremoniously canceled by Martin Goodman after only two issues.

Not even the venerable Captain was safe. With sales declining, Lee and his team did whatever they could to drum up new interest, even going as far as having Bucky shot, killed, and replaced by Steve Rogers's girlfriend, Betsy Ross. But the hero's brand of red-blooded, fist-swinging patriotism seemed old-fashioned to young readers growing up in the postwar boom. In July 1949, Captain America was discontinued.

In part, Lee realized, the shift in audience tastes had a lot to do with the rapid rise of television. In 1950, for example, fewer than four million American households had TV sets; the following year, the number jumped to ten million, and to fifteen million the year after that.[7] To keep up with the times, Lee rushed to produce replicas of the sort of stuff that was popular on the small screen, from sunstricken cowboys to hard-boiled detectives. He wasn't thrilled with most of it, but it hardly mattered—it was still a swell way to make a living.

It was also a good way to pay for the life Lee had always wanted, a life of perpetually making up for the deprivations of his childhood. He took a room at the Almac Hotel on Broadway and 71st Street, a nineteen-story dark-brick building that housed everyone from jazz musicians to visiting baseball players to Nazi scientists living under assumed identities and working on armaments for the United States government. He dated as much as he could, and enjoyed daily strolls to Timely's new offices in the Empire State Building. In his autobiography, he recalled these days as a string of happy coincidences and spirited pranks, from racing horses in Central Park to a brief and amicable relationship with a high-end escort who regaled him with tales of her clients' fetishes. He traded in his convertible, not the most practical car in New York winters, for a sedan, and took immense pleasure in driving his mother and aunt around town. He was still insecure about money, still a child of the Depression suffering from the lingering stress of want, and every bit of luxury was to be cherished, celebrated, and shared.

It was especially poignant that luxury be lavished on Jews, who just a generation or two before were newcomers struggling to feed themselves and their families. As much as he shied away, later in life, from anything that would tether him too tightly to the faith of his fathers, Lee seemed deeply aware that he was still, despite his success, an outsider looking in. One day, he was having lunch with good friend Ken Bald at Longchamps, an upscale restaurant known for its Art Deco design and its sparkly clientele. They were sitting outside when a bird flying overhead relieved itself, the droppings falling on Lee's shoulder. Without skipping a beat, Lee looked heavenward, shook his fist, and yelled in mock outrage: "For the gentiles, you sing!"[8]

But Lee's days as a fun-loving bachelor would soon end. One afternoon, a friend who was dating a model set Lee up on a date with one of his sweetheart's coworkers. Lee was supposed to meet her at the modeling agency, but when he showed up, another woman, also a model, opened the door. She was a gorgeous, red-headed Brit; desperate to wow her, Lee made up one of his fantastic stories. He was a comics creator, he told her, and he'd been drawing the same woman's face since he was a little boy. It was the woman he saw in his dreams each night, the love of his life. It was her face, and he was madly in love with her.

The conceit was so preposterous it made the woman laugh. She introduced herself as Joan Clayton Boocock, and the couple started dating. Two weeks later, Lee proposed. Boocock said she'd be happy to accept if she weren't already married. Stunned, Lee listened as his girlfriend told him much of her life story. She was a wartime bride, having married an American serviceman she'd known for only twenty-four hours and moved to the States. Her relationship with her husband soon fizzled, but she was, in the eyes of the law, still Mrs. Sanford Dorf Weiss. As divorce was a complicated affair in New York State at the time, Lee suggested that she travel to Reno, Nevada, which required only a six-week residency before granting a divorce. Boocock agreed and left for the West, promising to write Lee frequently. But when one of her letters arrived addressed to "Dear Jack," Lee, anxious that the gorgeous woman might decide to marry someone else, bought himself a last-minute, multistop, twenty-eight-hour plane ride that finally led him to Reno and to Joan. There he again told her that he loved her and insisted they get married right away. He found a judge and persuaded him to annul Joan's marriage in one room of the courthouse, and then, walking into the room next door, to officiate their wedding.

Returning to New York, Lee, not much of an observant Jew, nevertheless felt the need to have the union blessed again, this time by a rabbi. The newlyweds moved across the park to a large apartment on the Upper East Side. Two weeks later, on December 16, 1947, Lee's mother, Celia, died of stomach cancer. Realizing that his father was not capable of raising his younger brother Larry on his own, Stan stepped in, moving the fifteen-year-old in with him and his new bride. Despite the responsibilities of caring for a teenager, Stan and Joan made the most of that period, throwing dinner parties and enjoying their two cocker spaniels, Hamlet and Hecuba. Two years later, they moved from the city to a cottage on a 1.2-acre property featuring its own duck pond in exclusive Hewlett Harbor, Long Island. In 1950, their daughter, Joan Celia, was born.

All this domestic bliss more than made up for a career he no longer found particularly compelling. The comics industry, still booming, was now producing a wide variety of titles, from schlocky monster stories to lurid tales of crime to salty light erotica, and Martin Goodman's business strategy revolved around flooding the market with as many of these titles as he could possibly produce. Knowing that he could trust Lee to deliver decent quality copy on time, he allowed his star editor the freedom to do more or less what he wanted.

Lee made good use of Goodman's trust, working from home twice a week and, in the summer, writing on his front porch with his feet in the small, circular plastic pool he'd bought for his child. But after a few years, he began to feel like his life was getting repetitive. "Go to the office," he described his routine during what he would later call his limbo years, "come home and write—weekends and evenings. Between stories, go out to dinner with Joanie, play with little Joanie, look at cars."[9]

To keep himself invigorated, he turned back to the one hero he'd always most enjoyed reinventing: Stan Lee. After *Writer's Digest* featured him on a cover of a story titled "There's Money in Comics!," Lee decided it was time to further boost his legend by self-publishing a magazine entitled *Secrets Behind the Comics*. He sold it for a dollar, ten times the price of a comic book. The first "secret" was Lee himself: featuring a glamorous headshot of the writer in a bow tie, a pencil behind his ear, the introduction—written by Lee himself—sang Lee's praises and then promised to rub off a bit of his magic on the reader: "NOW, for the first time ever in the world, Stan Lee will show you exactly how comic strips are WRITTEN!!!"[10]

With greater fame, however, came greater pressure. From time to time, Goodman, whose editorial philosophy involved copying other publishers' successful titles and ripping them off with minor changes, asked Lee to contribute to one of the men's magazines that made the company most of its fortune. Lee agreed, terrified of losing his job, but the industry, he observed, was heading in a dangerous direction. Back in the 1940s, it had been dominated by the existential dread of first-generation American Jews who invented characters that embodied and dispelled their worst fears, from economic ruin to genocide, while keeping squarely within the Protestant ethos that had always driven American culture. A decade later, however, there was no trace of anything quite so elevated: comics were a mass market bloated by cash and fans and publishers willing to try anything to make a splash. Some of the crime titles were way too gory for Lee's taste, and some of the romance titles too titillating. Comic books were drifting farther and farther away from anything the precocious kid who had once spent his days reading the classics could defend. It was probably the reason he took criticism of the industry so readily to heart: he was incensed when new acquaintances wrinkled their noses when he told them he was a comic book writer, perhaps because he shared more than a bit of their distaste for what comic books had become.

Seeing comic books as an instrument of moral degradation was a view as old as comic books themselves. No sooner had Superman taken flight than John Francis Noll, the bishop of Fort Wayne, Indiana, rose to warn his flock against the twin dangers threatening the American way of life: Communism and comic books. The latter, he thundered, were "an evil of such magnitude as to threaten the moral, social and national life of our country," the work of publishers whose "diabolical intent" was "to weaken morality and thereby destroy religion and subvert the social order."[11] You could forgive the industry's creators, the overwhelming majority of them Jews, for hearing a trace of the ancient hatred in Bishop Noll's rants against shadowy figures hell-bent on corrupting pure Christian souls. But whereas anticomics rhetoric remained limited to a few vocal critics in the 1930s and 1940s, by the mid-1950s the mainstream press had joined in, and the anticomics movement was ready for someone to step in and lead it into the limelight.

That honor fell to Fredric Wertham. Despite his Bavarian roots, the psychiatrist intimately understood the fascinations and machinations of his adoptive American culture. In 1934, while serving as an expert witness in a murder trial, he had shocked the courtroom by launching into a speech about how all expert testimony, his included, was tainted by self-interest. His little outburst earned him a few favorable headlines, and he soon took to writing true-crime accounts of famous real-life murders with titles like *Dark Legend* and *The Show of Violence.* As committed as he was to his medical practice, he was blinded by the appeal of celebrity, and he began looking for the next path into the front pages of the papers. Comic books seemed like a natural step.

In 1948, the writer Judith Crist published a five-page article about Wertham's work, titled "Horror in the Nursery." The headline's sensational tone was sustained throughout the piece: Wertham's findings, Crist wrote, "constitute a warning to the parents of the nine out of ten American homes into which the comic books eventually find their way." In case the words were too ambiguous, the article featured an illustration showing a young boy pinned to the floor by a young girl while another child stabbed him with a fountain pen.[12] Anticipating any criticism his anticomics advocacy might engender, Wertham told Crist that freedom of speech was no excuse for endangering the well-being of the young. "We are dealing with the mental health of a generation," he said. "If those responsible refuse to clean up the comic-book market—and to all appearances most of them do, the time has come to legislate these books off the newsstands and out of the candy stores."[13]

Crist's article couldn't have been more favorable to Wertham, but soon he realized that he could generate even more attention if he wrote his own articles. These led the way to his book, *Seduction of the Innocent,* published on April 19, 1954, by Rinehart. Two days later, the Senate Subcommittee on Juvenile Delinquency devoted a hearing to Wertham's ideas. Well armed with examples of the industry's worst transgressions, the committee's investigator, Richard Clenenden, kicked off the proceedings by showing the gasping senators a stack of gruesome titles, including one about an eight-year-old girl who shoots her father and frames her mother for the murder, and another about an abused wife who chops up her alcoholic husband with an axe and stuffs his body into liquor bottles. Wertham testified, too, as did a number of comics publishers. When William Gaines, Max Gaines's son and the publisher of EC Comics, was called to the stand, he was shown the cover of one of his publications, featuring a woman's decapitated head. "Do you think that is in good taste?" asked Senator Estes Kefauver of Tennessee. "Yes, sir, I do," Gaines replied, "for the cover of a horror comic."[14]

The committee concluded its session the following day—coincidentally, the same day Senator Joseph McCarthy launched his hateful inquiry into the possible Communist infiltration into the U.S. Army—and adjourned until the summer. But the industry wasn't about to wait for the government's official censure. Instead, a number of publishers got together to create the Comics Magazine Association of America, whose first act was to deliver a Comics Code governing what comic books could and couldn't depict. It was, its creators boasted, "a landmark in the history of self-regulation for the entire communications industry."[15]

Most comic book creators, however, were feeling less chipper about this newly imposed onus of censorship, and, true to an industry that thrived on heroes and villains, they relished portraying Wertham as a menace. In this pastime, Lee was unsurpassed. One of his stories from the period, titled "The Raving Maniac," featured Lee himself, engaged in an argument with a man who was clearly modeled after the crusading psychiatrist. The stranger delivers a frothing rant against comics, and Lee, in a move straight out of an old Captain America comic, pushes him into a chair and delivers a sparkling monologue about freedom of speech. "In a dictatorship," he says, "people try to change your mind by force! You should be grateful you're in a land where only words are used!"[16] As the story ends, readers are treated to one final twist: the man, we learn, was insane, an escapee from the local asylum. In the comic's final panels, Lee puts his daughter to bed, telling her a bedtime story about the "excited little man" he'd met earlier in the day.

But for the time being, the excited little man had prevailed, and constant considerations of just what the Code might approve made Lee's days a little more miserable. They soon got much worse when Goodman, after a string of miscalculations, found himself locked in a bad distribution deal and, shuffling off to Florida, ordered Lee to fire the entire staff. Moved to a small cubicle, and constantly contemplating quitting, Lee gathered a skeleton crew of freelancers and did his best to keep the business running.

He was plagued by personal, as well as professional, woes: in 1953, Lee and Joan had a second daughter, Jan, who died a few days after her birth. To recover from the tragedy, the couple tried to adopt a child, but soon found that most adoption agencies, traditionally run by religious organizations, refused to work with an interfaith couple. This incensed Lee, who thought belief should bring people together, not set them apart. But it was too hopeless a battle for him to fight, so he threw himself back into his work, managing the handful of artists he could afford to hire.

Among them was Jack Kirby. The previous thirteen years hadn't been kind to the talented artist, who found himself booted by DC and abandoned by Joe Simon, who had quit the industry altogether and taken a job with an advertising firm. Strapped for cash, Kirby overcame his distaste for Lee and took whatever work his former errand boy could throw his way. When Lee pitched an idea for one last Hail Mary comic book, a superhero story like never before, Kirby figured he had nothing to lose.

5

The World's Greatest Comic Magazine!

WORKS THAT PROFOUNDLY RESHAPE their medium and culture at large—think *Citizen Kane* or *Sgt. Pepper's Lonely Hearts Club Band*—present us with a challenge of interpretation. How to approach a monument already imbued with so much meaning? How to understand a human creation now thrust into the realm of the eternal? In the case of *The Fantastic Four*, any attempt at illumination must begin with process.

For the most part, the comic book industry, driven almost exclusively by volume, fashioned itself after that other bastion of industrious immigrant Jews—the garment business. Shops were set up where artisans toiled for little pay, overseen by bosses who grew wealthy by hustling for an ever-growing share of the market. This sort of logic prized productivity above creativity, which meant that bosses considered it best to set up an assembly line that moved along smoothly and rapidly. For virtually every publisher, this meant a writer coming up with a detailed story and passing it along to an artist to illustrate, a perfectly bifurcated system that allowed for flexibility whenever necessary, as writers and artists could be pulled from one project and parachuted into another on a moment's notice. Even the great ones, even those who'd created the industry's iconic, best-selling heroes, were afforded no special treatment, and most did their own inking—filling in the color after sketching the frame with a pencil—and their own lettering, adding the text to each frame. A tailor, went the industry's logic, was only a tailor, and even the best ones were easy to replace. For the most part, comic book artists were never credited, and you had to be an insider to know who did what.

Even before he began working on *The Fantastic Four*, Stan Lee thought differently. Maybe it's because he was never really a comic book geek at heart and saw himself not as a master of the medium but a convener of great talent and a conductor of symphonies; maybe it's because he was, unlike so many others who crammed the cubicles of comic book publishers, a well-read man with aspirations to high culture; or maybe it's because he realized that his greatest creation, Stan Lee, would be well served if flanked by the industry's top talent. Whatever the reason, Lee considered his artists to be partners in the creative process, none more cherished than Kirby.

How did their relationship work? John Romita Sr., another of Lee's favorite artists, recalled one typical chaotic conversation. He was in a car with Kirby and Lee, driving from Manhattan to Long Island. The conversation turned to the plot of *The Fantastic Four*. Lee talked excitedly, shooting off ideas just as fast as they entered his brain. Kirby waved his stubby cigar in the air, parrying with ideas of his own. It took Romita a long while to realize that the two weren't actually listening to each other. "They would both come in with their ideas," he said, "they would both ignore each other. . . . I never really knew which way they would go because both of them had a different aspect on the story."[1]

This unorthodox way of working allowed for more than just diverse and interesting story lines. It made for an entirely new kind of comic book, one that contained multitudes and could explore new emotional and moral depths previously unthinkable in a medium originally geared toward the young. To understand why, just look at the Talmud.

With the Romans occupying the land of Israel, and with Judaism imperiled by a host of conflicts and threats, some external and others internecine, the rabbis who led the community faced the unprecedented challenge of securing the survival of their faith. Their task grew even more dire after the sacking of Jerusalem in 70 c.e.; for nearly a thousand years, Jewish life had been centered around the rituals conducted in the Temple, and now that it was destroyed the rabbis had to reimagine Judaism and reinvent it as a religion that could survive even after its beating heart was burnt. Their solution was radical: put it all in a book.

How to do that was an infinitely more complicated question. The first instinct, one can imagine, might have been simply to write down all the laws and the traditions, leaving behind a clear codex for future generations to consult. But such an approach came with one key peril. Confine the laws in that way, and they become a series of edicts to either embrace or reject. Such an arrangement, the rabbis knew, was much too strict for most people. Even the faithful didn't relish blind obedience, and a religion that was not much more than a strict list of dos and don'ts wasn't likely to remain vibrant for long. Instead, they came up with a strange and wholly original structure: they would leave behind not invocations but conversations. Read a page of the Mishnah, the first collection of laws redacted in the third century c.e., or the Gemara, later analysis and commentary on the Mishnah—together, the two are often referred to as the Talmud—and you'll find that it is, to quote the poet, stuffed with the stuff that is fine and stuffed with the stuff that is coarse. One moment, the rabbis may be debating what's to be done if you buy a ship and find precious cargo inside; the next, they're telling a fantastic story about a favorite biblical character before diving into yet another discussion about this tradition or that. The most striking feature of this book thick with wonders is just how frequently these learned men disagree. This, too, is by design: the earliest compilers of the Mishnah were known as the Zugot, or the Pairs, two wise rabbis often matched up precisely because they saw the world in starkly different terms. The best known among them are Hillel and Shammai, the former lenient and kind and the latter imperious and strict, their arguments still parsed and studied by each new generation of observant Jews.

Built this way, the Talmud guarantees that any newcomer to the text will be merely the latest partisan in an argument spanning two millennia. This is why Talmud is traditionally studied in small groups of peers—disagreements, often animated, are essential not only to the experience of study but, really, to the theological understanding itself.

This earthbound logic of contentious coexistence between irreconcilable differences is evident from the very first pages of the first issue of *The Fantastic Four*. Their story begins dramatically, with a flare gun that spells the group's name going off, causing the people in the street below to panic. Soon, we learn that the gun was fired by a shadowy man standing at the window. Or, not exactly: he is, Lee announces in his characteristic breathless style, "somehow more than just a man—for he is the leader of . . . The Fantastic Four!"[2]

Like the baffled New Yorkers watching the scene unfold, readers, too, are introduced to the Fantastic Four by seeing them in action and in reaction to the world around them. Sue Storm, the Invisible Girl, darts through the city, terrifying passersby by doing ordinary things like paying for a cab ride or elbowing her way down a crowded city block while transparent. Two years before Betty Friedan wrote of the problem that has no name, Storm already proved that the problem, the profound unhappiness of women struggling to live meaningful lives in an often dismissive patriarchal society, had no face as well. But even if you weren't inclined to see her particular power as a metaphor for the erasure of women from public life, you could still enjoy the pages, drawn with Kirby's signature kinetic frenzy.

But if Sue Storm is invisible, Ben Grimm has the opposite problem. We first meet the Thing as he's futilely trying to buy some clothes that fit him. The shop, naturally, doesn't carry anything in his monstrous size, so the flare gun signal comes as a relief. Stomping down the street, he spooks a few policemen who, without thinking, draw their guns and open fire. The Thing rips open a manhole cover and jumps into the sewer; Kirby stops the action to give us one haunting panel of a blue, curvy, watery tunnel with only the Thing's head and fingers peeking out, a tortured expression on his face, a reminder that the mighty giant may be stronger than anyone on Earth yet feels the pain of his alienation. Finally, Johnny Storm, Sue's kid brother, is fixing his hot rod in a garage when he sees the signal. He flames on and flies through the skies as the Human Torch, but first has to avoid a handful of fighter jets whose pilots mistake him for a missile. His flame begins to die down, and he plunges, limp and helpless, to a certain death, only to be rescued in the very last moment by Reed Richards, Mr. Fantastic, stretching his body to catch the falling boy. We're then treated to a brief telling of the Four's origin story—led by Richards, they embarked on a clandestine spaceflight, hoping to single-handedly beat the Communists to the punch, and were exposed to cosmic rays that altered their molecular structure and turned them into their enhanced selves—and then, the bickering begins.

Jealous of Sue's love for Richards, the Thing, only a moment after his terrible transformation from human to creature, tears down a tree trunk and swings at the scientist, who is shocked to learn that his limbs are now endlessly elastic, wrapping an arm tightly around the raging hulk and keeping him from doing more harm. Both men, then, stumble upon their superpowers only when they choose to fight with each other, and the fight remains the engine that propels them forward.

"Listen to me, all of you!" Richards says gravely when he and the Thing both calm down. "Together we have more power than any humans have ever possessed!" For emphasis, Kirby has Richards deliver the line against the inky black sky, lit by the golden glow of his burning spaceship. Then the color scheme turns naturalistic again, and it's the Thing's turn to speak. "You don't have to make a speech, big shot!" he says. "We understand! We've gotta use that power to help mankind, right?"[3]

Like the ancient rabbis, the Thing and Mr. Fantastic routinely offer up divergent ways of looking at the world. The reader's pleasure derives, in large part, from trying to figure out with whom to side. It's never a foregone conclusion—unlike previous heroes, who were understood to be the supreme source of their universe's moral authority, the Four are notably human and explicitly devoid of any one transcendent light to guide them.

What is the quarrel between the Thing and Mr. Fantastic really about? The obvious answer is that they represent brain and brawn, the two elemental forces that power all human affairs. One of them is a brilliant and verbose scientist; the other made of hard, orange rock. It's a particularly tempting explanation given the Jewish identities of their creators, Kirby and Lee. One, the artist, was the son of poor immigrants who clawed his way out of poverty by kicking and punching alongside the members of his gang; the other, the writer, was the son of poor immigrants who clawed his way out of poverty by reading and writing his way to the editor's chair. If you're inclined to see the world through a narrow socioeconomic prism, you can see the

Thing as a street Jew—the kind of tough who, if he got lucky, might have gone on to do well in business—and Richards as a book Jew—the sort of egghead who found fame and fortune by practicing medicine or law.

But *The Fantastic Four* is a more nuanced work than that, and it defies expectations from the very first pages. Richards may be a brilliant scientist, but it was his colossally careless miscalculation and his hubris that turned the four into mutants to begin with. And the Thing may be the world's strongest creature, but he is, as he lets us know when he floats despondently in the sewer, vulnerable and lonely. He's also fiercely intelligent, being the sole member of the team to have objected to the ill-fated mission to space and the only one who accurately predicted the deleterious impact of those otherworldly rays. These nuances are a sharp departure from the monochromatic world of 1950s sci-fi, in which anxieties over new and potentially destructive technologies and the machinations of the Cold War gave birth to a parade of aliens, UFOs, ray guns, and other madcap creations. And they have presented generations of critics with a conundrum: just how to read *The Fantastic Four*, or, for that matter, all of Lee's oeuvre? What is the creator of a comic book universe thick with mighty yet flawed beings trying to tell us about our own spiritual condition? Or is there no larger message, nothing more than colorful panels and alliterative writing and cool characters that fight each other ad infinitum?

It didn't help much that the master himself was, as ever, playfully elusive: whenever he was asked about the real meaning of this character or that plotline, Lee—taking a page from another gnomic Jewish artist, Bob Dylan—mirthfully shrugged off any attempt at earnestness, leaving his readers to offer theories of their own.

While frustrating for anyone trying to write a biography of Lee, say, this constant flight from anything concrete has served to make Lee's work infinitely more interesting: his comic books, like Dylan's songs, have become vast cultural canvases onto which anyone interested in the art form can paint her or his own interpretations, an ongoing dialogue with the artist that mirrors the ancient Talmudic logic of constant conversation and disputation. This, in part, may explain the staying power of Lee's work: the pleasure it offers lies not in attempting to empirically prove that a certain character ought to be read only a certain way, but in reaching into the cornucopia of culture and pulling out all the pieces that seem to fit in Lee's expansive universe.

This is a particular pleasure—or frustration, depending on one's point of view—for Jewish critics, who have spent decades and spun a small cottage industry arguing about just what the new mythologies constructed by American Jewish artists owe to the old ideas of their ancient religion. Here, again, little by way of indisputable proof offers itself easily: we know, for example, that Lee attended synagogue habitually as a child, that he celebrated his Bar Mitzvah, and that he was active in his synagogue's drama club, but none of the above is sufficient to confer on him any rabbinic-like familiarity with or passion for Judaism's texts or traditions, or to suggest that we ought to read Lee's comic books looking for traces of scripture. But knowing Lee's background, and detecting so many allusions to otherworldly forces in his work, frees the reader to seek to understand Lee's creations by planting them in a Jewish context and seeing whether they fit. And the rivalry between the Thing and Mr. Fantastic does, as both heroes represent deeper archetypes rooted in the very soil of Jewish mysticism.

The Thing is a golem. Even though Jewish lore is packed with tales of creatures made of dust or clay—Adam himself is one, a mighty giant shaped out of mud and kissed by God with the breath of life—the best-known dates back to the sixteenth century, when Prague's Rabbi Judah Loew fashioned himself a creature out of the dirt of the banks of the Vltava River. The golem—the Hebrew word means "misshapen mass"—was powerful not only physically but spiritually as well, and had the power to see men's souls and summon the dead. When he got out of hand, his creator destroyed him by removing one of the Hebrew letters placed in his mouth as part of the incantation that animated him, changing the Hebrew word *Emet*, or truth, into *Met*, or dead.

Like the golem, the Thing has a complicated relationship with his creator, Richards. Like the golem, created to protect the Jews from their persecutors, he is unimpressed by the maniacal foes that threaten his friends anew in each volume. And like the golem, he is more soulful than one would expect, often seeing right through the intricate emotional tangles that keep the other three from being true to themselves.

Modeled after Kirby himself, the Thing was always imagined as Jewish, even though he wasn't explicitly identified as such until 2002. In one of the most marvelously introspective masterworks of comics—created by Karl Kesel and Stuart Immonen and cleverly titled "Remembrance of Things Past," after Proust's opus—the Thing mills about his old neighborhood. He's convinced that it's Yom Kippur, and wants to atone for stealing a Star of David necklace from a local pawnbroker named Sheckerberg decades ago, when he was a boy. The necklace was Sheckerberg's prized possession, the only thing in his shop that wasn't for sale, and the young Ben Grimm stole it as a rite of passage required by his street gang. Remorseful, he finds Sheckerberg, but the pawnbroker, it turns out, is being squeezed by an extortionist named Powderkeg, who, true to his name, sets off a bomb that throws the pawnbroker to the ground. Believing Sheckerberg to be dead, the Thing stands above his body, and, admitting that "it's been a while," recites the *Shema*, arguably Judaism's most seminal prayer, in Hebrew.

Sheckerberg regains consciousness and is moved by the Thing's prayer. "It's good, too, to see you haven't forgotten what you learned at temple, Benjamin," he says. "All those years in the news, they never mention you're Jewish. I thought maybe you were ashamed of it a little?" The Thing shakes his head. "Nah," he replies, "that ain't it. Anyone on the Internet can find out, if they want. It's just . . . I don't talk it up, is all. Figure there's enough trouble in this world without people thinkin' Jews are all monsters like me." They chat for a while longer, and then Sheckerberg states the obvious. "Remember the tale of the golem, Benjamin? He was a being made of clay . . . but he wasn't a monster. He was a protector." As the story draws to an end, Sheckerberg gives the Thing the Star of David necklace, figuring even a modern-day protector needs protection of his own.[4]

Part hero and part cautionary tale, the Thing, again like the golem, is a constant reminder that the few and the chosen will always be persecuted by their enemies, that they will often need to defend themselves forcefully, and that they ought to watch out, because the distance between truth and death is always just one letter away. These complexities make the Thing much more than a flawed and troubled hero in the mode of, say, Jack Frost. They make him into the embodiment of ecstatic truth, a figure who may be fictional but is too real not to truly exist. In this, he joins a long line of Jewish heroes; King David, the English diplomat Duff Cooper once observed, "must have actually existed, and most of it must be true, because no people would deliberately invent a national hero so deeply flawed."[5]

Richards, on the other hand, is a less obvious creature. As he first learns of his newfound elastic ability, he ponders out loud, "What am I doing? What happened to me?," sounding like a man possessed.[6] And he is: a close reading of Richards's actions and motivations place him squarely in another supernatural Jewish tradition, that of the dybbuk. Though the dybbuk is commonly understood today as an evil spirit entering the body of an innocent victim, its origins are more intricate, and they have to do with the surge in mysticism that accompanied the birth of the Hasidic movement. When the first Hasidic masters appeared on the scene in eastern Europe in the eighteenth century, in large part as a response to a Judaism that they believed placed too much of an emphasis on the law and not enough on the spirit, they sought to break through the conventional barriers of piety and worship God in new and ecstatic ways, which often included chanting, dancing, and other physical pursuits. Observing their actions, their critics frequently derided them as mad, but madness, these masters retorted, was really nothing more than trying to transcend. A man who seems possessed by a spirit may simply be a man in possession of a soul so exalted that it casts away mundane things like reason and attempts instead to cling to the divine. The term they sometimes used to describe this condition was *devekut*, Hebrew for adherence. There is, the scholar of Hasidism Zvi Mark wrote, "a substantive comparison between the condition of *devekut* and that of madness fomented by a dybbuk. In both cases, the subject loses control and is taken over by a foreign existence that invades or resides within him or her, determining the person's actions. Both conditions are characterized by a disconnectedness from the surrounding environment."[7]

A scientist, Richards isn't content with merely doing his work in the traditional context of universities and research institutions. He's a nuclear age Hasid, eager to get closer to his source and unlock all the mysteries of his field of knowledge. "No time to wait for official clearance!" he tells the others as they sneak into the spaceship Richards had been busy building for the government.[8] While his destination, in Stan Lee's original memo, was Mars, in the published comic book events took a turn for the metaphysical: "Before the guard can stop them," the caption reads on a panel showing the rocket blasting off into outer space, "the mighty ship which Reed Richards had spent years constructing is soaring into the heavens . . ."[9]

He continues to display the same devekut, the same zealous quality, in volume after volume, looking increasingly like a man possessed. While the others have traces of a social life—the Thing and the Human Torch horse around, and Sue Storm, by far the group's most intelligent and well-balanced member, does her best to keep the boys grounded—he is frequently shown locked in his lab, working on some contraption or another that never seems to come to fruition. This, really, is one of the comic's finer jokes: allegedly the smartest man in the world, Richards invents a host of doohickeys—a flying car! A swell, fortified pad for the four on top of a skyscraper!—but never anything that might bring real redemption to the world. The Thing, again, is quick to call him out on it. In one adventure, for example, Richards scolds his burly colleague for interrupting his scientific work—the Thing had merrily snuck up on the Human Torch as the teenager was showering, turning up the hot water to a maximum and making the startled Johnny Storm flame on and fill the apartment with smoke. "I'm in the middle of a new rocket fuel experiment which is almost reaching fruition, and I've got to interrupt it also!" Richards says in his usual cumbersome manner of speech. "Big deal!" the Thing replies. "We already got rocket fuel, haven't we?"[10]

The Thing isn't wrong, and in his frustration Richards doubles down on his efforts. It's no coincidence that the Four's greatest enemy is Dr. Doom, a former classmate of Richards's who, like him, is obsessed with obtaining godlike knowledge but who, unlike Mr. Fantastic, is willing to turn to dark magic to meet his goals. Richards and Dr. Doom aren't that different, which is what makes the iron-masked villain so terrifying. Under slightly different circumstances, he might've joined the gang; now, he's there not only to set evil traps but also to teach Reed Richards the lesson anyone possessed by a dybbuk must learn, the lesson of humility and repentance.

The old Hasidic masters, fond of telling stories, left behind tale after tale of dybbuk possessions that end only once piety had been restored. Usually it's the dybbuk itself, a lost and wandering spirit, who must correct its ways before enjoying a restful afterlife; fluent in *gilgul neshamot*, or the transmigration of souls, the rabbis in these stories identify the dybbuk's previous lives and the sins that led it to its demonic form and then guide it as it mends its ways and rejoins the fold of the righteous. Reed Richards is a more complicated case, as he's possessed by a dybbuk of his own making: it was his vanity and impudence that drove him to space, where his body was seized by some foreign spirit that now commands it in ways that Richards can neither understand nor fully control.

Always humming in the background, the theme of possession took center stage in *The Fantastic Four* number 10, which remains one of the most beloved comic books in the series. It features Jack Kirby and Stan Lee as themselves—an indication of how popular their new comic book has become in less than a year—receiving a visit from Dr. Doom. Previously seen drifting off into space after having failed again to defeat the Fantastic Four, the masked menace returns with a vengeance, armed with what he calls "mystic science," which he learned from an alien race he'd met called the Ovoids. Among their chief virtues is the ability to switch souls, a dybbuklike move that enables them to ease into new bodies whenever their old ones grow tired. Using this strange new power, Dr. Doom switches bodies with Mr. Fantastic, then hatches a plan to destroy the Fantastic Four from within. Like a good Hasidic tale, the possession ends only when the dybbuk humbly repents, showing his innate goodness to his friends and convincing them that he's the real Reed Richards even though he's trapped in Doom's hideous body.

Like the Thing, modern-day golem, the dybbuk that is Mr. Fantastic should be read, at least in part, as a warning. Arriving at the dawn of the space race, he is there to remind us that our appetite for discovery, blessed and healthy as it may be, should always be curbed by the recognition that we will never unfurl the truly cosmic mysteries, the ones reserved for the divine. It is a call for goodness over greatness, one not always easy for a nation in the throes of a Cold War to hear.

Yet as the sixties rolled on, it was just the sort of wake-up call that resonated all around. Instead of love-me-dos, the Beatles, for example, were soon exploring more elevated plateaus; asking the recording engineer to route his voice from the recording console into the studio's speaker on "Tomorrow Never Knows," John Lennon explained that he wanted to sound "like the Dalai Lama and thousands of Tibetan monks chanting on a mountain top."[11] When he spoke, a little while later, about being bigger than Jesus, he wasn't just being cheeky but was expressing, accurately, his desire to capture the old spiritual energies that were now more likely to animate rock 'n' roll bands than the tired clergy of poorly attended synagogues and churches.

The Fantastic Four got there first. Long before guitar players and filmmakers and painters and just about anyone else doing anything creative began to challenge the old Protestant paradigm of modernity versus fundamentalism—an unhelpful paradigm in a world awash in both—Lee and Kirby, two Jewish boys, delivered a universe, a lot like our own, that was infinitely more intricate and compelling. Rather than champion this pole or that of a dichotomy that was too extreme and inhospitable for actual human beings—no one, after all, is utterly a modernist reformer or completely a fundamentalist zealot—they created a world in which the best human beings could hope for was not deliverance by some god in tights but the hard, communal work that makes life just a little bit better. And they reminded readers that using too much force and having too much faith were two sides of the same treacherous coin; the path to redemption, if there was one, required humility, camaraderie, and sacrifice, not traditionally qualities associated with omnipotent superheroes in comic books.

Of course, you hardly had to see the immense depths of

The Fantastic Four to enjoy the work. Always an artist of distinction, Kirby rose to new heights with the series, like a latter-day Goya capturing the vicissitudes and torments of the suffering human soul. When Dr. Doom, for example, is foiled in his attempt to possess Mr. Fantastic, Kirby gives us a close-up of the villain, framed against a shocking red background, with an expression on his face that captures, for one fleeting moment, the hurt and pain of a man who has devoted his entire life to a cause and must now watch it fade away.

If the faces were rich with feeling, however, the backgrounds were constant reminders that *The Fantastic Four* answered to a higher calling. Using black fractals as negative space amid sizzling fields of color exploding in red or yellow or orange blotches, Kirby created an effect known as the Kirby Crackle. Without resorting to a single word, it informed the readers that they were experiencing something beyond a mere childish plot, something closer to an ecstatic revelation. "For Kirby," one critic later wrote, "the human body is a manifestation or crystallization of finally inexplicable energies—a superbody. . . . What Mesmer called animal magnetism, Reichenbach knew as the blue od, and Reich saw as a radiating blue cosmic orgone becomes in Jack Kirby a trademark energetics signaled by 'burst lines' and a unique energy field of black, blobby dots. . . . The final result was a vision of the human being as a body of frozen energy that, like an atomic bomb, could be released with stunning effects, for good or for evil. These metaphysical energies . . . constitute the secret source of Kirby's art."[12]

And, as always, there was Lee's particular genius for mythmaking. Some of it was right there on the page. Most adventures began with the Four lounging in their swanky headquarters, feet on the sofa, trading insults before rushing to reluctantly work together and save the world. With time, their bickering grew darker, with Sue Storm, for example, developing feelings for the Sub-Mariner after he leapt to the Four's aid against the nefarious Dr. Doom, a complication that put her engagement to Reed Richards in peril. But much of Lee's magic was evident in what can only be called the metaphysics of marketing: crowning the Four the world's greatest comic, or inserting himself and Kirby into the story, unabashedly signaled to the readers that they were entering a new pantheon, one populated by new gods who will not disappoint.

The readers agreed. Letters came pouring in by the hundreds. All talk of retirement was abandoned. A short while after *The Fantastic Four* debuted, and without even seeing the sales figures, Martin Goodman—who had changed his company's name from Timely to Atlas and then to Marvel—rushed to Lee and asked him for more of the same, and right away. But Lee had other ideas.

6

❖◆❖

I Don't Need You!

How to follow up a smash hit like *The Fantastic Four?* Comic book history provided Lee with a clear blueprint: do the same thing, with slight variations. Martin Goodman was hoping for another team of lovable, bickering heroes, each with his or her own flaws.

"I still recall Martin's expression after he asked how many heroes I'd put in the next team," Lee later wrote in his autobiography. "You should have seen the look on his face when I told him the next series wouldn't feature a team. There would only be one superhero. Oh, and by the way—I wanted that hero to be a monster."[1]

As always with the strategically dissembling Lee, it's hard to know precisely what inspired this insight. According to one theory, reading *The Fantastic Four*'s fan mail, Lee noticed that most of the love went to the Thing: as blunt with his feelings as he was with his fists, the rocky giant was the group's id, his resentiments and desires rarely sublimated, making him the group's most emotionally accessible member. Yet the new hero Lee would soon create would possess none of the Thing's brute charm. A scientist turned into a monster by the might of his own invention, he was brooding and secretive when human and imperiously dismissive when turned into a beast. Unlike Frankenstein's monster or Quasimodo—other sources of inspiration frequently cited by Lee—there was nothing of the misunderstood misfit about Lee's new creation. Even his skin color, a sepulchral gray, was designed to suggest that the Incredible Hulk belonged in some other, metaphysical realm.

The story is set in New Mexico, reimagined by Jack Kirby not so much as a state but as a state of mind. The very first panel introduces a landscape that is either busy being born or busy dying, all cracked earth and sharply jutting cliffs, awash in the sort of beige you can imagine the world might've been before the creation of color. In the middle of this scene protrudes a light-blue space age divining rod. It is, Lee's typically energetic caption informs us, "the most awesome weapon ever created by man—the incredible G-Bomb!"[2] Two panels later, we meet its creator. He is framed, in Kirby's inspired touch, by the window of the fortified bunker in which he's sheltered, waiting for the weapon he'd made to be tested. He is Dr. Bruce Banner, genius scientist, and we first see him sucking on a pipe with a distant, slightly troubled look on his face. Behind him stands another frowning man. "I was against it from the start, Banner, and I still am!" he says. "It is too dangerous!"[3]

Soon, we are launched into a very different drama from any that had ever plagued Mr. Fantastic and his crew. It's one of petty office politics. The naysayer, Igor, continues to badger Banner, arguing that so devastating a contraption ought to have been examined by a team of scientists rather than by just one physicist, no matter how brilliant or proud. Banner hardly has time to respond when General Ross barges in: supervising the

G Bomb project for the army, he's impatient to try it out, and he criticizes Banner and his colleagues for being too cautious. Weapons, he barks, ought to be controlled by soldiers, not bespectacled nerds. He makes a sympathetic point, as does Igor; the only one who seems designed to repel our empathy is Banner himself. When Igor, for example, tries one more time to plead with the physicist to share his secrets—"If you've made an error, you might blow up half the continent!!" he shouts—Banner looks at him coolly and answers, "I don't make errors, Igor."[4] Anyone wishing for the arrogant scientist to get his comeuppance doesn't have to wait long: as the countdown for the test begins, Banner spots a teenager driving across the test site. He rushes out to save the boy's life, instructing Igor to delay the bomb's launch. Igor does no such thing, and Banner, having had just enough time to toss the boy into a nearby protective ditch, absorbs the radiation of the mighty and mysterious gamma rays. He screams for hours, traumatized and anguished, but as night falls, he grows into his monstrous alter ego, the Incredible Hulk.

What happens next is far less clear. More, perhaps, than any of Lee's characters, the Hulk was subject to deep and essential changes as the series progressed. His skin, for example, soon turned green—largely because Lee and Kirby discovered that comic book printers, working with basic machines and cheap paper, were unable to consistently produce the Hulk's pale gray, making him sometimes pitch black and sometimes off-white. More important, his essence soon morphed as well, turning him from a Mr. Hyde–type beastie who turned big and bad each nightfall like clockwork to an immensely more complex creature who began to morph from Banner to Hulk only if the former failed to control his anger.

"Needless to say (but I'll say it anyway), *The Incredible Hulk* . . . was enthusiastically received by the fans," Lee wrote later, "and we had another winner on our hands."[5]

That, sadly, was far from the truth, or at least the literal truth. The Hulk was canceled after only six issues. With exact sales figures unavailable for many months, Goodman must have pulled the plug based on the reaction of his famous gut, which probably told him that the new hero was just too strange ever to make it big. Indeed, years later, when Lee and Kirby restored the Hulk to a series of his own, he became a hit predominantly with a very small subset of college students, who saw him as the sort of antihero the counterculture of the late 1960s could celebrate. This gave the green giant some cachet, and a second chance that proved sufficient for survival. But read these original issues, and you'll understand just how radically Lee was progressing as an artist, and just how ambitious—and biblically inspired—his vision had become.

With *The Fantastic Four*, Lee had rejected the tired old drama of Protestant America, that of fundamentalism versus modernism, the source of so much dreary culture. He and Kirby replaced it with a more audacious dichotomy, that of golem versus dybbuk, the former a call to perpetual, sometimes violent, vigilance and the latter a lesson in humility and a reminder that the greatest mysteries of existence aren't ours to solve. Theirs was no longer the first-generation immigrant's anxious fantasy, sublimating the values of their host nation and responding by slapping tights and a cape on the embodiment of their own insecurities, a magical immigrant from space who can fly but who must keep his true self hidden from the suspicious gentiles. Instead, however self-consciously, they delivered a profoundly Jewish vision and watched a spiritually unmoored America embrace it with enthusiasm. And now, it was time to take things a step further. In Lee's telling, the Hulk wasn't humanity's protector, nor was he, like Frankenstein's monster, the embodiment of humanity's hubris. He was, really, humanity itself, struggling to make sense of the terrors and beauties of its own being.

How best to understand a creature tasked with such an

onerous undertaking? Jekyll and Hyde, naturally, come to mind, but unlike the protagonists of Robert Louis Stevenson's tale, Banner and the Hulk aren't pure good and pure evil personified. In fact, they are a double helix carrying various facets of the same matter, and they are interchangeably strong and weak, wise and foolish, gallant and malicious, all depending on the circumstances. To best understand this intricate dichotomy, one needs to consider the lonely man of faith.

The term comes from a 1965 essay by Rabbi Joseph B. Soloveitchik, a Jewish philosopher so singularly influential that he was known simply as the Rav. The nature of modern man's dilemma, he wrote, can be summarized in three painful words, which both Banner and the Hulk might have embraced as their motto: "I am lonely." That, Soloveitchik went on to argue, was almost by design. If you wanted to understand that empty feeling that haunts so many of us, he advised, just look to the story of creation.

Or, rather, the stories of creation: the first two chapters of Genesis present us with two versions of how we humans came to be, neither compatible with the other. "So God created man in his own image," the Bible's very first chapter informs us, "in the image of God created he him; male and female created he them. And God blessed them, and God said unto them, Be fruitful, and multiply, and replenish the earth, and subdue it: and have dominion over the fish of the sea, and over the fowl of the air, and over every living thing that moveth upon the earth."[6]

Soloveitchik called this creature Adam the First. His motto, he observed, is *Imitatio Dei*, the man who aspires to be godlike by constantly creating new things and reshaping his world in his image. "The most characteristic representative of Adam the First is the mathematical scientist," Soloveitchik wrote, "who whisks us away from the array of tangible things, from color and sound, from heat, touch, and smell which are the only phenomena accessible to our senses, into a formal relational world of thought constructs, the product of his 'arbitrary' postulating and spontaneous positing and deducing."[7] Always asking how and never why, this Adam "transcends the limits of the reasonable and probable and ventures into the open spaces of a boundless universe."[8]

He is, in short, Bruce Banner. It's not in vain that we meet the brilliant scientist engaged in skirmishes with his colleagues—for Adam the First, the whole world's a workplace. This is why, in this telling, we've not one human being delivered at the dawn of time but two, a man and a woman, partners in labor and in glory. "The two are better than the one," Ecclesiastes informs us, "because they have a good reward for their labor. For if they fall, the one will lift up his fellow; but woe to him that is alone when he falleth, and hath not another to help him out."[9] But whenever there are two, there is also a struggle for recognition, respect, status, power; Banner, a classic Adam the First, toils to find balance between competition and collaboration, an alienating pursuit if there ever was one.

Enter Adam the Second. For some reason that's never really explained, no sooner does Genesis deliver one account of creation than it rushes to offer a second one, entirely contradictory to the first. "And the Lord God formed man of the dust of the ground, and breathed into his nostrils the breath of life; and man became a living soul," we are told. "And the Lord God took the man, and put him into the garden of Eden to dress it and to keep it. . . . And the Lord God caused a deep sleep to fall upon Adam, and he slept: and he took one of his ribs, and closed up the flesh instead thereof; and the rib, which the Lord God had taken from man, made he a woman, and brought her unto the man. And Adam said, This is now bone of my bones, and flesh of my flesh: she shall be called Woman, because she was taken out of Man. Therefore shall a man leave his father and his mother, and shall cleave unto his wife: and they shall be one flesh."[10]

Among the many variations in this second, strange account of creation, two stand out. First, God does not create man and woman together but shapes Eve out of Adam's rib. And second, man is not given dominion over the world—an invitation to re-order it in his image—but is rather appointed its conservator and custodian, a mindful caretaker commanded to "dress it and keep it." Adam the Second, then, isn't interested in achieve-ment. Instead, his are more metaphysical concerns. Enmeshed in a more intimate relationship with his Creator, he wants to better understand the terms of their otherworldly conversation, in which one side, God's, is present but forever silent. "Adam the Second," Soloveitchik noted, "keeps on wondering: 'Who is He who trails me steadily, uninvited and unwanted, like an everlasting shadow, and vanishes into the recesses of transcen-dence the very instant I turn around to confront this numinous, awesome, and mysterious 'He'?"[11]

That bit of imagined monologue, elevated as it may be, could have been delivered by the Hulk. In the first issue's most heartbreaking moment, the gray colossus, having just escaped the army's grip, wanders in the desert, wondering where to go next. Some dim recollection leads him to a row of bungalows; he identifies the third among them as the place that is calling him, although he cannot begin to remember why. When he enters it, we understand what the Hulk doesn't: it's Bruce Banner's home. There, he has a short altercation with Igor—unsurprisingly for the period, the Slavic-named colleague turns out to be a Soviet spy—that culminates with the Hulk crushing Igor's pistol in his enormous hand, mocking the technological advancements that the industrious humans—all those Adam the Firsts—so revere. When the fight is over, however, the Hulk is back to his brood-ings. "Bruce Banner!" he moans, "Why do those words stay in my head?? What is that name to me??"[12]

The question is the distillation of the series' real drama. The Hulk/Banner is interesting not because of his plotlines—

unlike the Fantastic Four, he was never provided with an operatic nemesis like Dr. Doom, and the struggle of his split persona meant that no real human relationship was possible for either the Hulk or Banner—but because of his existential struggle. One part of him wants to focus on worldly achievements, on advancement, on career; another sees that there's more to life, vying for the sort of redemption that comes only when you spend every waking hour trying to get closer to the mysteries of your creation.

Is it any wonder, then, that the Hulk eventually found an attentive audience in college students nationwide? The central question of his being is one that the young, still struggling to make sense of the meaning of it all, obsessively entertain. It is the question of loneliness, and how to be in the world if you're unwilling to succumb to its crushing weight and admit that not only is it not possible for you to know your fellow man or woman, but that even knowing yourself is an uphill battle.

Soloveitchik offered a radical answer to this conundrum. Rather than Adam the First's community, a transactional tribe based on mutual interests and subject to the sort of imminent disappointments you feel when you discover that a member of your group, say, was a Soviet spy all along, he proposed the kind of community erected by Adam the Second, the covenantal community. In this arrangement, human beings look not only to other human beings but also to God: by themselves, Adam and Eve are just two lonely people, as unable to communicate as any other two. With God in the picture, they are elevated, transformed, partners in a three-way process that gives them rhythm and meaning. They become not merely partners in production but friends, a sacred term.

To enter into this blissful arrangement, however, the two Adams must realize that they are one and the same, and that the internal struggle between them is eternal. They must recognize that they are both the inherent parts of creation, and that a human being is never complete if he or she struggles to be only one kind of Adam or the other. Still, the two are frequently locked in conflict, which, in the mid-1960s, seemed as bitter as it had ever been: Adam the First, now possessing the knowledge to travel to space and construct bombs that could destroy the planet, appeared more conceited than ever, impatient with Adam the Second and his irrational ways. And Adam the Second, in response, seemed prone to skid into zealotry and call on his spiritual powers to punish the wicked materialists, an instinct shared by a handful of radicals later in the decade as they rushed to bomb and shoot what they perceived to be a sinful establishment. The Hulk sounds like a member of the Weather Underground *avant la lettre* when, holding a snapshot of Banner, he howls, "Fool! I am glad it happened!! I'd rather be me, than that puny weakling in the picture. I don't want you with me! I don't need you! I don't need anybody!"[13]

But he does, and Banner needs the Hulk just as badly. This uneasy codependence works itself out with the help of two other participants, Rick Jones and Betty Ross. The first is the teenager whose life Banner saved at the test site; an orphan, he decides to dedicate his life to serving his benefactor. In another dig at the sidekick trope he so dearly despised, Lee made him not the wide-eyed youth whose sole job is to gawk at the hero's marvels but a level-headed young man who is entrusted with the impossible task of explaining the Hulk to Banner and Banner to the Hulk, a peacekeeper toiling to piece together the hero's deeply fractured self. The same is true of Ross. She is the daughter of the general who resents Banner his brilliance, which means, naturally, that she is in love with the tortured genius of a scientist. She feels sparks of the same infatuation whenever the Hulk appears, which baffles her, a confusion not in the least aided by the fact that neither the physicist nor the brooding beast seems capable of spending more than a few minutes in her presence before inexplicably disappearing. The story of the series is the story of all these people learning to come together in a covenantal relationship, accepting the mystery of creation—in this case, Banner's rebirth as the Hulk—and learning to love and support one another despite grappling with so much they can neither understand nor control.

Which isn't really the sort of stuff that had traditionally kept caped crusaders up at night. Writing about the Hulk years later, one critic wondered out loud just what was the point of the Green Giant: "It all added up to pure misery for the title character, filled with blackouts, fear, guilt, and unrequited love for the general's daughter Betty. You could call the Hulk a super-hero, but what was he saving? And from whom?"[14]

These questions proved overwhelming even to Lee himself. By 1963, a year after the Hulk's appearance, he was preoccupied not only with his work but with his larger creation, the myth of Stan Lee. A gossip column from the time captured the manufactured glamour that Lee sought to project, casting himself as the sophisticated editor at the heart of a rapidly changing media landscape: "A gay poolside party and buffet supper Saturday evening was hosted by Writer–Art Director Stan Lee (Lieber) and his beauteous British-born wife, Joan, at their 125 year old Colonial home on Richards Lane," it read. "Always decorative, Mrs. Lieber, her blond tresses piled high, received in a long black and white checked gingham dishabille du soir caught at the waist with a cluster of daisies. The interesting, attractive and talented company included David Mansure, painter here from Columbia, S.A., on a Guggenheim Fellowship; Magazine Publisher Martin Goodman and his wife Jean; Mr. and Mrs. Kenneth Bald (he's the artist for the Dr. Kildare Comic Strip); TV Commercial Announcers Kay Dowd and Stanley Sawyer . . ."[15]

But as Lee was lounging by the pool, a new generation of college students was diving deep into his work. By 1965, the Hulk made *Esquire* magazine's list of the twenty-eight people most revered on the nation's campuses, alongside John F. Kennedy and Bob Dylan. "Marvel often stretches the pseudo-scientific imagination far into the phantasmagoria of other dimensions, problems of time and space, and even the semi-theological concept of creation," one Cornell student said while expressing his love for the Hulk. "They are brilliantly illustrated, to a nearly hallucinogenic extent. Even the simple mortal-hero stories are illustrated with every panel as dramatically composed as anything Orson Welles ever put on film."[16]

The Hulk, however, wasn't the only one of Lee's creations to make the list. Another, newer hero did, too, even more unlikely than the scientist turned monster. He was, perhaps, Lee's greatest and most memorable creation, a teenager learning about power, responsibility, and free will.

7

With Great Power

IN MARTIN GOODMAN'S WORLD, credit always had a short shelf life. As long as his long-suffering editor was delivering moneymaking hits, the publisher was happy to give Lee a bit of freedom to experiment. But with the Hulk fizzling, Goodman instructed Lee to deliver a more traditional superhero, the sort that was more about action and less about brooding. By then, Goodman, flush with cash, was spending two or three hours each day in his office, playing Scrabble with a good pal he'd hired as his business manager. Not one to openly challenge his employer, Lee let his resentment simmer. There he was, an artist in full, having just delivered, with *The Fantastic Four,* a masterpiece that he believed had changed comics forever, and there was Goodman, behaving like it was still the fickle forties and rushing out a torrent of schlock. Goodman, Lee told an interviewer decades later, "felt comics were really only read by very, very young children or stupid adults. He didn't want me to use words of more than two syllables if I could help it. . . . Don't play up characterization, don't have too much dialogue, just have a lot of action." It was, Lee added, "a job; I had to do what he told me."[1]

And Goodman's instruction to create more superheroes struck Lee as troublesome. The publisher, he knew, thought in terms of trends: just as there had been a flurry of western-themed comics, followed by romance and monsters and hard-boiled detectives, he considered superheroes the flavor of the month, a craze to be exploited until it faded away. But Lee was already convinced that superheroes were more than passing distractions; they were the protagonists of new American dramas, scripted by Jews whose emotional lives were scarred by the Great Depression and the Holocaust and the desire to make a life for themselves by doing more than merely aching to assimilate by playing up Protestant fantasies. These dramas were the ones America, traumatized by decades of hardship and war, was slow to recognize; years before its popular entertainers grappled with power and justice and responsibility, Lee's light-footed fleet of heroes assailed these themes in short, declarative sentences in thin volumes millions of young adults read eagerly each month. All of that was lost on Martin Goodman, however, and Lee wasn't about to let his life's work go to ruin. To save it, he did something he had never attempted before: he deliberately defied his boss.

Ignoring Goodman's call for more heroes that looked and felt just like the Fantastic Four, Lee spent months thinking about his next character. Slivers of insight came to him one by one: he ought to be young; he ought to be poor; he ought to be ambitious; he ought to be the sort of guy who just knows that he's destined for greatness, but who finds himself on the margins of society, struggling to get recognition and respect; he ought to be powerful but still deeply vulnerable, never entirely in command of the complex circumstances of his life. In short, he ought to be a lot like Stan Lee. But what sort of superpower should he have? And what to call him? Once Lee had figured out the answers to these questions, he walked in to Goodman's office and pitched his idea.

His new hero, he told his boss, would be called Spider-Man. His alter ego, Peter Parker, would be a teenager bitten by a radioactive arachnid and blessed with great strength and agility. The name, Lee went on, had come to him while watching a fly buzz about the office one day. "I can't remember if that was literally true or not," he confessed in his autobiography, "but I thought it would lend a little color to my pitch."[2]

Goodman hated it. People, he told his editor, hated bugs; flies and spiders were for squashing, not revering. And the main hero couldn't be a teenager—teenagers were sidekicks and nothing more. Warming to his subject, Goodman went on, telling Lee that he was describing, really, a comedic character, not a fearsome warrior ready to take on the world's most evil villains. And with that, Goodman clicked his tongue a couple of times and went back to his game of Scrabble.

At any other turn in his long career, it's likely that Lee would have obeyed, forgetting all about Spider-Man and returning with another concept the boss considered more commercially viable. But the Fantastic Four and the Hulk seemed to have rubbed off on their creator; like them, he was powerful and misunderstood, forever fighting to save an ungrateful society from itself. The new comic, Lee resolved, would see the light of day, if only once. Goodman, he knew, was terminating a series called *Amazing Fantasy* after fourteen lukewarm issues. The fifteenth and last, Lee decided, would feature Spider-Man. If the boss ever found out—doubtful, as the title was already en route to oblivion—Lee could always apologize and say he didn't think it mattered, this being the swan song of both *Amazing Fantasy* and his teenaged, web-slinging hero.

Working at his habitually frantic pace, he asked Jack Kirby

to sketch the new hero. Parker, Lee told his artistic collaborator, should look like the kind of kid who might suffer from allergies and the occasional bout of acne. But after decades of buff he-men, Kirby couldn't help himself, and delivered a guy who was too blond, too broad-shouldered, and too cheerful to pass as the milksop Lee had in mind. Lee needed another artist to realize his character. He turned to Steve Ditko.

The son of Slovak immigrants—his father was a carpenter at a steel mill, his mother a homemaker—Ditko grew up in Johnstown, Pennsylvania, and spent most of his waking hours reading comic strips. In high school, with World War II having just erupted, he built models of German warplanes, to help aircraft spotters back home point out a Stuka should one materialize over the Allegheny Mountains. He enlisted as soon as he could, was shipped off to Germany, and spent the war drawing comic strips of his own for army publications. Single-minded, he took his GI Bill money after the war was over and moved to New York to study at the Cartoonists and Illustrators School. There, under the tutelage of Jerry Robinson, one of *Batman*'s best-known artists, he spent two years attending classes five times a week for five or six hours at a pop, working hard on honing his skills. He received assignments from a host of imprints, including Joe Simon and Jack Kirby's, before arriving at Lee's office in 1955 and asking for work.

It hardly took Lee's singular gift for spotting talent to notice that there was something sublime about Steve Ditko's art. Whereas Kirby's backgrounds crackled with energy and detail, Ditko's were often monochromatic, blank backdrops stressing that the real drama was happening inside the character's mind. Having spent a long period in his youth struggling with tuberculosis, he was accustomed to seclusion—he would eventually spend much of his adult life as a recluse. And, turning his considerable powers of observation inward, he could capture operatic emotions in one single curve of a character's eyebrow or dip of a villain's lip. When he saw the sketches Kirby had created for Spider-Man, he knew his colleague had gotten it all wrong.

Inspired by his own earlier work, Kirby had imagined Spider-Man as a sort of Captain America redux, giving him the same half-face mask, underwear-and-tights combo, and in-spired emblem emblazoned on his strapping chest. Ditko wasn't enthusiastic. "One of the first things I did was to work up a cos-tume," he said years later in a rare interview. "A vital, visual part of the character, I had to know how he looked, to fit in with the powers he had, or could have, the possible gimmicks and how they might be used and shown, before I did any break-downs. For example: A clinging power, so he wouldn't have hard shoes or boots, a hidden wrist-shooter versus a web gun and holster etc." The key to understanding the character's emo-tional stance, however, was the mask: "I wasn't sure Stan would like the idea of covering the character's face but I did it because it hid an obviously boyish face. It would also add mystery to the character and allow the reader/viewer the opportunity to visu-alize, to 'draw,' his own preferred expression on Parker's face and, perhaps, become the personality behind the mask. Did it work that way? (There are interesting psychological theories about masks.)"[3]

The psychological, philosophical overtones were another Ditko staple. By 1962, he had become an adherent of Ayn Rand's Objectivist worldview. He was also sharing an apartment off Times Square with Eric Stanton, a renowned fetish artist who specialized in scenes of bondage and female dominance, occa-sionally helping his roommate complete some of his racy draw-ings. He brought all these preoccupations into his work when he sat down to imagine Spider-Man, giving him a web-print mask in red and blue, with large, white eyes lined in thick black, like some kind of Kabuki mask. Whatever the psychological theories Ditko had in mind when he sketched his newest hero, the effect was just as he had hoped: to look at Spider-Man's blank eyes was to feel not only his pain and insecurity but your own as well, like an abyss you stare into long enough only to realize that it, too, is staring into you.

More than anything else, it was this eerie blankness that was most prominent when *Amazing Fantasy* number 15 was finally released in August 1962. The cover was illustrated by Kirby—Lee still didn't trust Ditko to capture the drama of the new hero, and had him merely ink the more senior artist's work—but even though Spider-Man ended up with a bit more muscle than Lee would have preferred, it was his empty glare that was most arresting, not the fact that he was swinging on a web or holding a startled criminal under his arm. This emotional ambiguity called for a different style of storytelling, one that would replace Lee's habitual breathlessness with something more intricate and nuanced. From the very first page, Lee hit just the right note.

"Like costume heroes?" he asked, addressing his readers directly. "Confidentially, we in the comic mag business refer to them as 'long underwear characters'! And, as you know, they're a dime a dozen! But, we think you may find our Spiderman just a bit . . . different!"[4] The scene that unfurled below was just as antithetical to anything previously seen in a comic book: A gaggle of attractive teenagers, speaking in the prickly staccato of the hormonally young, are mocking a peer, Peter Parker, who is standing to the side, thin and forlorn. He is leaning on a side panel featuring the silhouette of a man and a spider, like something out of a movie by Murnau. The breaking of the fourth wall, the Expressionist game of shadows juxtaposed with the sunny high school scene, the smiling teens standing next to the sorrowful Parker—all those foreshadow the fact that the dramas about to unfold would revolve around moral decisions, and that the reader would be called upon to engage emotionally with the story in ways previously untested by the medium.

The rest of the story delivers on these promises. Parker, an orphan, lives with his Uncle Ben and Aunt May. He is smart and hardworking, which makes him an outcast with the cool kids. Instead of going to the dance, he rushes off to a science exhibit, where he is bitten by a radioactive spider. Stumbling outside, he discovers that he now possesses the arachnid's powers, including great strength and the ability to scale buildings. He sews himself a spider costume, complete with concealed contraptions that sling strong webs, then turns to the obvious pursuit for someone of his newfound skill set: show business.

"Now anybody with the intelligence of a seven year old knows that if a man appeared on TV who seemed to be more spider than human, he'd be an overnight sensation!"[5] Lee wrote in the opening of the comic's second act, featuring Spider-Man showing off for the cameras and admired by an awestruck audience. If the Fantastic Four wrestled with celebrity as a side effect of their powers, the young Peter Parker understood his might as little more than a conduit for fame and fortune. Scorned and rejected for too long, he was now eager to craft a new identity focused on his might. So when a robber zooms by, having just mugged someone, Parker refuses to intervene. "What's with you, mister?" the elderly police officer giving chase asks Parker after the baddie had fled to safety. "All you hadda do was trip him, or hold him just for a minute!" His Spider-Man mask delivering its empty stare, Parker is unmoved. "Sorry, pal!" he says, "That's your job! I'm thru being pushed around—by anyone! From now on I just look out for number one—that means—me!"[6]

Spider-Man grows more celebrated, but one evening, as Parker returns home, he's told that his beloved uncle has been murdered by a burglar. Enraged, he puts on his costume and tracks the killer to an abandoned warehouse; when he finally captures him, he is shocked to discover that it's the same man he himself had failed to stop a few days earlier. For the first and last time in the series' history, we see Parker's eyeballs piercing the dead white of the Spider-Man mask, a terrifying panel that delivers the full weight of the character's pain and guilt. Spider-Man ties up the murderer in a thicket of webs and delivers him to the police; then, Peter Parker rips off the mask and weeps. "My fault—all my fault!" he sobs. "If only I had stopped him when I could have! But I didn't—and now—uncle Ben is dead . . ." In the story's final panel, we see Parker in long shot, stooped and sad, walking under the pale moonlight. "And a lean, silent figure slowly fades into the gathering darkness," Lee wrote in one of his finest bits of prose, "aware at last that in this world, with great power there must also come—great responsibility!"[7]

It was hardly an original sentiment. "For unto whomsoever much is given, of him shall be much required," Jesus tells his disciples, "and to whom men have committed much, of him they will ask the more."[8] In 1906, Britain's newly appointed undersecretary of state for the colonies, Winston Churchill, resurrected this idea when discussing the empire's responsibilities to its faraway charges. "In some cases," he said, "we have great and overwhelming power of intervention, in other cases we have hardly any power of intervention at all. I submit respectfully to the House as a general principle that our responsibility in this matter is directly proportionate to our power. Where there is great power there is great responsibility, where there is less power there is less responsibility, and where there is no power there can, I think, be no responsibility."[9] And on April 11, 1945, just one day before he died, Franklin Delano Roosevelt turned to the same coinage in an address on Thomas Jefferson. "In Jefferson's time," he wrote, "our Navy consisted of only a handful of frigates—but that tiny Navy taught nations across the Atlantic that piracy in the Mediterranean, acts of aggression against peaceful commerce, and the enslavement of their crews, was one of those things which, among neighbors, simply was not done. Today, we have learned in the agony of war that great power involves great responsibility."[10]

But it was Lee's introduction of the sentiment, not Churchill's or Roosevelt's, that stuck: the phrase, often erroneously attributed to Uncle Ben, would go on to become a staple of American culture, quoted by everyone from President Obama admonishing China in a press conference to Justice Elena Kagan in a Supreme Court decision pertaining to intellectual property disputes. It resonated because, unlike its predecessors, it was not uttered by the mighty as a reminder of noblesse oblige but by an everyman trying to figure out the foundations of moral behavior. In Lee's telling, Spider-Man wasn't just another superhero trying to fathom the complexities of superhuman abilities; he was a young man learning how to be human, a direct descendant of the first biblical figure who wrestled with this very question: Cain.

As we first meet the farmer, in chapter four of Genesis, he, like Peter Parker, is a sullen loser: for reasons that are never explained, God has rejected Cain's offerings while gladly accepting those of Abel, his brother. "And Cain was very wroth," the holy book continues, "and his countenance fell. And the Lord said unto Cain, Why art thou wroth? And why is thy countenance fallen? If thou doest well, shalt thou not be accepted? And if thou doest not well, sin lieth at the door. And unto thee shall be his desire, and thou shalt rule over him."[11] God's advice is even more cryptic in the original Hebrew, which seems to have a word or two missing, confounding commentators for millennia. What is it, exactly, that the Almighty is advising Cain to do in his moment of sorrow?

According to most interpreters, God's words could be read in two ways. The first is a simple if/then proposition: if you do good, the Lord will accept you and embrace you, and if you fail to do good, you are sure to sin. But the Hebrew original suggests a second interpretation, one in which God warns Cain that whether he chooses to do good or not, sin lieth at the door regardless, always there to tempt mankind. Life, then, isn't about charting a course to happiness by choosing good over evil but about understanding that we cannot determine the circumstances of our lives, only our reactions to the woes that befall us. Our job, then, is to learn how to rule over our desires, our frustrations, our rage. And Cain fails this test miserably a verse later when, ignoring God's warning, he strikes his brother and kills him. "Here," Rabbi Joseph B. Soloveitchik wrote in his commentary on the story, "sin results not from arrogance, but rather from self-negation. This type of sinner is subservient to everything and everyone. He is a spiritual wanderer—he does not want to sin, yet submits to temptation; he wants to repent, but feels that he cannot; he senses the call of holiness, but does not answer."[12] This being the case, God curses Cain, but does not destroy him. When the sinner finally breaks down, saying "my punishment is greater than I can bear," God condemns him to a life of restless wandering but grants him the protection of a distinctive mark to shield him against the murderous urges of other fallen men.[13] The more cryptic interpretation of God's earlier warning is thus reinforced: both before and after committing his terrible crime, Cain must continue to grapple with the evil inclinations that crouch, like a wild animal, at his doorstep.

The same is true of Peter Parker. His aunt and uncle had urged him to stay humble, study hard, and follow his dreams, but his innate resentment—all those years of being laughed at by classmates who were more beautiful and more beloved—led him to succumb to the temptations of might, and, like Cain, suffer the consequences. His real struggle, then, would be not with a gallery of fantastic villains but with himself, the spiritual wanderer straining to hear and answer that holy calling.

That is, if he were to have any further travails at all: recalling Martin Goodman's stern rejection, Lee did not follow up on

Spider-Man. Once *Amazing Fantasy* number 15 was published, he and Ditko assumed that the character was to be no more, and went on to work on other titles. But soon the letters started pouring in, as many as a hundred in one day, all the writers proclaiming their love for Spider-Man and their eagerness to read more about his adventures. A few months later, a more substantial vindication followed: when the issue's sales figures were released, Spider-Man's debut turned out to be the best-selling comic book not only of the year but of the entire decade. Goodman, Lee recalled later, burst into the editor's office, smiling. "Stan," he boomed, "remember that Spider-Man idea of yours I liked so much? Why don't we turn it into a series?"[14]

In March 1963, *The Amazing Spider-Man*—Lee couldn't help gracing his creation with another adjective—hit newsstands nationwide. But if the first installment was a weighty tale of coming to terms with free will, temptation, and responsibility, what followed took a turn for the darker. Like Cain, Spider-Man was soon doomed to roam the world, chased by a cynical newspaper editor named J. Jonah Jameson, who is convinced the masked hero is a con man who isn't above orchestrating the crimes he then mysteriously appears to solve. The charge is particularly painful because it hits close to home: with Uncle Ben's death, Aunt May is forced to pawn her jewels, and a heartbroken Peter obsesses over finding ways to make money and help pay the bills. He decides to try out for the Fantastic Four, assuming that omnipotent superheroes must be paid handsomely for their troubles. After a long and entertaining sequence in which he breaks into their penthouse headquarters and battles each one, trading punches and insults, Spider-Man is distraught to learn that the Four are a nonprofit group, doing good for its own sake. He pursues another get-rich-quick scheme, which turns out to be a devious plot to frame him in a bit of Soviet espionage. By the end of the issue, he's again stumbling down a dark street, lamenting his fate. "Nothing turns out right," he sobs. "I wish I had never gotten my super powers!"[15]

It is an understandable reaction from a young man terrified of coming to terms with his responsibilities. Take away the mask and the colorful villains, and you can read Peter Parker's tale as an Ur-narrative of moral awakening: the child who succumbed to pride and resentment must learn to control his emotions and live up to his responsibilities to others. That, of course, is Cain's story, too: when God asks him about Abel, Cain replies, "Am I my brother's keeper?"[16] and the Lord, furious, answers in the affirmative: "The voice of thy brother's blood," God roars, "crieth unto me from the ground."[17] Humbled, Cain goes on to build a city, humanity's first urban dwelling. He is no longer permitted the bliss of living off the land, of being rooted in place—"When thou tillest the ground," God curses him, "it shall not henceforth yield unto thee her strength."[18] Instead, Genesis curiously informs us, he sires a long line of men and women who invent practices that imitate or sublimate the primeval experience of simply working the soil. From Cain's loins emerge Tubalcain, the world's first blacksmith, and Jubal, the world's first musician, giving us art and industry, a meager consolation prize for the essential connection we've lost, the connection with the motherly earth. And like their forefather, these descendants must learn to live with each other in crowded settings, tasked with the eternal challenge of correcting Cain's failing and coming to see themselves as true keepers of their brothers and sisters.

This idea animates the Spider-Man series from the very start. After a few more futile attempts to earn cash, Peter Parker comes up with a clever scheme: using his Spider-Man abilities, he will snap photographs of the villains he fights and sell them to Jameson for top dollar. With that, he becomes entangled with his nemesis, the first of many close connections he must

sustain and that deeply complicate his ability to keep his secret identity secret. Soon, for example, he falls for Betty Brant,
Jameson's secretary; when she's attacked by malicious gang-
sters, he's tempted to reveal his superpowers but ultimately
decides on a more cautious course of action, even though that
means appearing weak and helpless and failing to impress the
woman he loves, a high price to pay for his restraint. He's also
enmeshed with Flash Thompson, the beef-headed bully who,
at some point, puts on the Spider-Man costume as a prank;
Thompson ends up getting captured by Doctor Doom, requir-
ing the real Spider-Man to leap to the rescue. As the comic book
ends, Parker is again on the margins: the cocky Thompson
claims all the credit for the superhero's bravery. Lee ends one
of the early issues of *The Amazing Spider-Man* with Parker ago-
nizing. "Finally, alone in his room," reads the caption, "the
amazing individual called Spider-Man searches his soul, bewildered, confused, and bitter!" And Parker himself delivers an
emotional monologue: "Can they be right?" he wonders. "Am
I really some sort of a crack-pot, wasting my time seeking fame
and glory?? Am I more interested in the adventure of being
Spider-Man than I am in helping people?? Why do I do it?
Why don't I give the whole thing up? And yet, I can't! I must
have been given this great power for a reason! No matter how
difficult it is, I must remain as Spider-Man! And I pray that
some day the world will understand!"[19]

The world didn't understand, which made the series a
stunning success. To play up Parker's internal drama, Lee made
copious use of the thought bubble, a feature rarely used in the
action-oriented world of comic books at the time. After Spider-
Man suffers his first defeat—he is smashed by the powerful Doctor Octopus—we see him sitting in his room, his eyes closed,
his face a perfect mask of anguish. "I'm a failure!" he thinks
to himself. "Spider-Man is a joke . . . a nothing!" Aunt May,

meanwhile, stands in the background, framed by the door, having thoughts of her own: "Poor Peter's been moping in his room for hours! I wish he'd tell me what's wrong?"[20]

To further emphasize Peter Parker's haunted psyche and his struggle to become a moral man in full, Ditko continued to experiment. Soon he began packing the page with a nine-panel grid, a visual style that served to deliver a stark emotional effect. Reading the early Spider-Man comics as a child, Alan Moore, who would later go on to become one of the art form's most celebrated creators, said Ditko's dense pages added "a kind of claustrophobia, a kind of paranoia, to the work. His characters always looked very highly-strung. They always looked as if they were on the edge of some kind of revelation or breakdown. There was something a bit feverish about Steve Ditko."[21]

Lee noticed it too, but Spider-Man was soon much too popular for him to spend any time pondering his collaborator's state of mind. By November of 1963, he was confident enough of Spider-Man's potential for long-term success to announce, on the cover of the series' sixth issue, that "the Marvel age of comics is here!"[22]

The following year, indulging his talent for self-promotion, he proposed to Goodman that the company begin to market not only its characters but its creators as well. Marvel Comics, Lee realized, stood out because its publications took on the kinds of complex existential questions that its audience, college kids and teenagers, were themselves contemplating. Its readers expected not just mere escapist entertainment, but something deeper. They were looking to Marvel for the same validation they sought in rock icons or renegade literary figures like J. D. Salinger or anyone else they felt honestly embodied the spiritual tensions of the age. With that sort of attachment, Lee thought, just giving the artists credit wasn't enough; they had to be made into characters themselves, every bit as iconic as the superheroes they'd created. Never too subtle, Lee launched a

Marvel fan club, dubbed the Merry Marvel Marching Society, in November of 1964; members paid one dollar and received a letter, a membership card, a sticker, a button, and a scratch pad. They also received a one-sided 33⅓ vinyl record titled "The Voices of Marvel." On it, Lee couldn't resist poking fun at the reclusive Ditko, who, by that point, was barely present in the office, coming in only to drop off his work and then disappearing back into his home studio. Talking to Sol Brodsky, his production manager, Lee delivers the following dialogue:

LEE: Hey, what's all that commotion out there, Sol?
BRODSKY: Why it's shy Steve Ditko! He's heard you're making a record, and he's got mic fright. Whoops! There he goes!
LEE: Out the window again? You know, I'm beginning to think he is Spider-Man.
BRODSKY: You mean he isn't?

Ditko was asking himself the same question. He was irked by his minor clashes with Lee, particularly when the liberal-leaning editor would censor Ditko's antihippie quips, having Spider-Man express his support for an assortment of progressive causes instead. But what finally sent Ditko over the edge was an argument he and Lee had over the identity of the villain who had emerged as Spider-Man's greatest nemesis, the Green Goblin. Ditko wanted him to be just another stranger, a wealthy industrialist who develops the powerful serum that turns him into Spider-Man's monstrous tormentor. But Lee had other ideas. The whole point of Spider-Man, he knew, was his commitment, in the wake of Uncle Ben's death, never again to let down the ones he loves, even at the price of perpetual blows to his ego and his sense of well-being. This being the case, his bitterest enemy had to be someone he knew, forcing him into yet another fraught relationship that required sacrifice. The Green Goblin, Lee decided, would be Norman Osborn, the father of Harry Osborn, Peter Parker's best friend.

"Steve wanted him to turn out to be just some character that we had never seen before," Lee told an interviewer decades later. "Because, he said, in real life, very often a villain turns out to be somebody that you never knew. And I felt that that would be wrong."[23]

The Green Goblin's identity was slated to be revealed in issue number 39. Handing in issue number 38, which hit newsstands in the spring of 1966, Ditko also handed in his resignation. He would never illustrate another issue of Spider-Man again.

"Stan wouldn't have been able to stand it if Ditko did the story and didn't reveal that the Green Goblin was Norman Osborn," recalled John Romita Sr., who, being among the most talented artists in the Marvel bullpen, was tapped by Lee to take over the popular franchise. "I didn't know there was any doubt about Osborn being the Goblin ... Looking back, I doubt the Goblin's identity would have been revealed in *Amazing* #39 if Ditko had stayed on."[24]

To any other editor, losing a star like Ditko just as Spider-Man was ascending might've proved devastating. But if Lee felt any real sense of panic following Ditko's departure, he didn't show it. The method he'd forged with Jack Kirby, a partnership between writer and artist, was bigger, he was convinced, than any one individual, and allowed not only for creative freedom but also for a modular production process that enabled him to assign and reassign artists as needed. Besides, having been in the comic book industry long enough, Lee knew that today's trendy title may be all but forgotten tomorrow, and he didn't want to slow down just as his hand was getting hot. He saw himself as a gambler: "I was like a crapshooter rolling one great pass after another," he wrote years later. "You just don't stop when you're on a winning streak."[25]

But how to follow up a smash hit title that also was, or at least tried to be, a profound meditation on the human condition? The answer, Lee believed, lay not in the tormented souls of heroes but in the outside world, a world in which Medgar Evers had just been assassinated and Martin Luther King Jr., writing from his Birmingham jail cell, prophesied that "oppressed people cannot remain oppressed forever." For Marvel's next title, then, Lee and Kirby created not one hero but a schoolful of them, innocent youngsters who had been born different, yearning for freedom in a society that saw them as a menace.

8

◆◆◆

We Only Fight in Self-Defense!

FOR MOST OF THE SPRING of 1963, Lee and Kirby were busy working on a new series that would bring together a few of their best-loved heroes. Lee, in particular, was fond of crossovers—having Spider-Man meet the Fantastic Four, say, or face off against Doctor Doom—which he felt was both an effective way to differentiate the Marvel brand from its competitors and a useful storytelling device that made the heroes and their fictional universe feel more real. Once he had amassed enough popular characters, he banded them together in a supergroup called the Avengers: the Hulk was a member, as were a handful of new and promising heroes, including Thor, Iron Man, and Ant Man.

As entertaining as the new gaggle of good guys could be, however, and as good as it was as a vehicle for expanding Marvel's offerings, *The Avengers* was hardly an ideal venue for Lee to explore the themes and ideas that truly interested him. For that, he and Kirby came up with another series—this one, too, a get-together of several fantastically powered individuals. Lee wanted to call them the Mutants: the series, he explained to Martin Goodman, would revolve around a handful of young adults who were born with mutated genes that gave them extraordinary abilities. The publisher, however, was concerned that the word "mutant" was too obscure, and urged Lee to come up with a different name. If his heroes were to have extra powers, Lee eventually reasoned, it was only right to call them the X-Men.

To demonstrate just how different these heroes were from the rest of comicdom, Lee launched their inaugural issue by having their mentor, Professor Xavier, summon them using the power of his mind. The thought bubbles that were previously used to allow Peter Parker to vent were now moving the plot along, as the telepathic mastermind, bald and confined to a wheelchair, trained his young charges by dispatching deadly obstacles for them to overcome. This athletic demonstration of the young mutants' abilities was in lieu of an origin story, as the X-Men did not get their superpowers from a radioactive insect or from strange rays—they were born with them, members of an evolved species called *Homo superior*, the next evolution in the human genus.

Which, of course, meant that they were free of the psychological dramas that come with having to keep a secret identity secret, like Spider-Man, or negotiating, like the Fantastic Four or the Hulk, a transformation from being human to something other. Iceman, Cyclops, the Beast, and the Angel, Professor X's four students, were just being themselves, which made them every bit as light and comfortable in their own skin as Spider-Man was brooding and anxious in his. When a fifth recruit, an attractive red-headed woman, arrives at the posh Westchester County school, the four mutants behave like merry cads: trying to figure out what the new student's superpower may be, one of the mutants speculates it may be "the power to make a man's heart beat faster!" Rolling his eyes, his friend observes, "Y'know something, Warren, if I had your line, I'd shoot myself!"[1]

With little to direct their attention inward, Lee gave his heroes an external problem to face, another mutant named Magneto. Unlike Professor X and his benevolent bunch, Magneto and his Brotherhood of Evil Mutants aren't interested in peacefully coexisting with humanity. Instead, they wish to enslave it, a step they see as nothing more than the next step in history's natural selection. But rather than permit the rivalry to devolve into another showdown of uncontested good versus irredeemable bad, Lee and Kirby soon began to complicate the series with layers of nuance.

In *X-Men* number 5—written shortly after members of the Ku Klux Klan planted fifteen sticks of dynamite beneath the steps of the 16th Street Baptist Church in Birmingham, Alabama, killing Addie Mae Collins, Cynthia Wesley, Carole Robertson, and Carol Denise McNair, four innocent young African-American girls—the X-Men are confronted with the sort of deep-seated bigotry the comics' readers could witness every evening on the TV news. Professor X's students are sitting in front of the television, cheering for one of their kind as he dominates an athletic competition. After the mutant emerges victorious, the crowd boos him and pelts him with blunt objects, and the X-Men, watching in their school's spacious den, are appalled. "Look at the crowd!" says Angel. "They're livid with rage! Just like Professor X always warned us . . . Normal humans fear and distrust anyone with super-mutant powers!"[2] Confronted with society's violent distrust, is it any wonder that some mutants might want to rise up against humanity, by any means necessary? When one of Magneto's minions questions his decision to set off a bomb that would kill scores of innocent humans, the powerful mutant replies that a violent conflict is inevitable. "Have I not told you," he tells his associate, "they are merely *Homo sapiens*— they would kill us if they could! We only fight in self-defense!"[3]

It was difficult, reading the comic in 1963, not to see the rivalry between Professor X and Magneto as a reimagined version of the tense real-life relationship between Martin Luther King Jr. and Malcolm X. Even though his group announced itself as evil in its very name, Magneto was merely another solution to the very real problem of human prejudice. "I did not think of Magneto as a bad guy," Lee said years later. "He was just trying to strike back at the people who were so bigoted and racist. He was trying to defend mutants, and because society was not treating them fairly, he decided to teach society a lesson. He was a danger, of course, but I never thought of him as a villain."[4] Still, Lee made sure readers never felt too fond of the vengeful mutant: when Magneto succeeds in taking over a small nation, he props up an army of goose-stepping thugs, complete with armband insignia, proof that violence, even in the service of a defensible cause, could only ever beget more violence.

But even as Lee and Kirby were writing what many critics, at the time and thereafter, believed was their civil rights parable, the reality of the movement was changing. It hardly took a political scientist to figure out that the bond between African-Americans and American Jews—cemented by Rabbi Abraham Joshua Heschel's marching with Dr. King in Selma and by Andrew Goodman's and Michael Schwerner's dying alongside James Chaney in Mississippi—was evolving into something very different. The Student Non-Violent Coordinating Committee (SNCC), for example, once a paragon of black and Jewish cooperation—Howard Zinn was an early mentor—voted, in 1966, to exclude all whites from its leadership, resulting in the forced departure of a number of prominent Jewish activists. A year later, the group published a fierce attack on Israel, illustrated by a cartoon of a Palestinian and an African-American both hanging from nooses held by a hand adorned with a Star of David. Disgusted, the actor and folksinger Theodore Bikel, previously an active supporter of SNCC, wrote a letter denouncing all affiliation with the group.

"I shall continue to be part of the civil rights movement and to be active in it," read Bikel's letter. "But I shall choose to fight on the side of those who, like Dr. Martin Luther King, speak with the voice of sane and deliberative determination; who believe that this is a movement to unite men as brothers, not divide them by the litmus test of color; who seek not to establish one kind of supremacy doctrine in place of another, but who concentrate instead on the fight against the real enemies—poverty, ignorance, and hatred of fellow-man."[5]

This atmosphere of disillusionment, of bonds broken and fear on the rise, permeates every page of the early *X-Men* series. In one memorable issue, for example, Dr. Bolivar Trask, an anthropologist who believes mutants to be a threat to mankind, constructs a species of robots, called the Sentinels, to protect humanity against the mutant threat. Professor X challenges Trask to a debate, trying to convince him that the mutants want nothing more than peaceful coexistence with their *Homo sapiens* brothers and sisters, but Trask is unmoved, unleashing his robotic guardians. Soon, however, the cyborgs develop a consciousness of their own, and, capturing their creator, demand that he build more and more Sentinels. They also force Trask to build a machine that can read mutant minds, and when the Beast is captured, Trask learns that, contrary to his fears, the mutants had never meant mankind any harm. Sacrificing himself, Trask blows up the Sentinels, setting free humans and mutants alike. As the X-Men wonder just what had happened, Lee concludes the story line with the following note: "Perhaps the truth will one day be known! But, until that time, it lies buried beneath countless tons of rubble—buried in the breast of Dr. Bolivar Trask, whose last earthly sacrifice brought the work of a lifetime crashing down about him—whose last earthly lesson proved to be: beware the fanatic! Too often his cure is deadlier by far than the evil he denounces!"[6]

The story line highlights what Danny Fingeroth, veteran Marvel writer and editor, argued was at the heart of the X-Men franchise, the idea that "any harm an individual does should be blamed not on that person's group, but on the personal choices he or she makes." It's the same subtext, he wrote, that animated Spider-Man and the Hulk, "but *X-Men* takes the metaphor a step further by being about *groups* (persecuted or not) in conflict with each other, as opposed to *individuals* being targeted."[7]

Yet Lee's preoccupations—the spiritual stirrings that guide individuals to right or to wrong—were never far from the surface. In issue number 12, Lee and Kirby introduced Professor X's backstory, a tale laden with some of Lee's favorite themes. Born Charles Francis Xavier in New York City, Professor X was the only son of Dr. Brian Xavier, a brilliant and wealthy nuclear scientist, and his wife, Sharon. After his father dies in a freak accident, his mother marries Kurt Marko, the late Dr. Xavier's business partner. Marko is abusive and manipulative, particularly when it comes to his own son, Cain Marko. An arrogant, apish man, Cain storms into the Xavier mansion demanding money and accusing his own father of causing the accident that killed his partner. A fight breaks out in Marko's lab, and an explosion follows. With his last shreds of life, the elder Marko saves both boys from the fire, then confesses that he hadn't done all that he could have done to save the elder Xavier's life. Before he dies, he warns the young Charles Xavier about his stepbrother: Cain, he says, will stop at nothing to destroy Xavier, particularly once he finds out about his sibling's mutant powers. As the comic book unfurls, we're treated to a few more horrifying instances of abuse, with Cain Marko—the pun on Mark of Cain couldn't have been lost on many—trying to hurt, and, in one instance, kill his younger sibling. Finally, while serving in the Korean War, Cain stumbles on the ancient lost temple of Cyttorak, site of a mighty and enchanted ruby. Rubbing it, he acquires its mystical powers and transforms into the Juggernaut, an invulnerable monstrosity who can chop up mountains with his bare hands and requires neither food, water, oxygen, or rest to persist. With the help of the X-Men—as well as a guest appearance by the Human Torch—Professor X finally triumphs over his menacing brother, but even in his moment of victory he maintains a note of sadness and compassion. "If things had been different," he tells the vanquished Cain, "we might have been friends . . . we might have truly been brothers!"[8]

The introduction of Cain Marko is only one instance in which the series veered from civil rights metaphor to intensely Jewish drama. In another, earlier occurrence, Magneto, talking to his associate, the Scarlet Witch, reminds the young woman of their first meeting. "Have you forgotten that day, not long ago," he says, "when I first came to your village in the heart of Europe? Have you forgotten how the superstitious villagers called you a witch because of your mutant powers?"[9] Kirby's haunting illustration featured a terrified young woman, running from a burning hut, while in the foreground hideous-looking peasants sneered at her, holding pitchforks. Coming eighteen years after the liberation of Auschwitz, this scene—Lee makes sure we know it took place in "the heart of Europe," not in some fictitious or unnamed place—left little room for the imagination, but just in case anyone missed the allusion to the Holocaust, Lee and Kirby followed up with another powerful panel: holding the traumatized young woman in his arms, Magneto reminds the Scarlet Witch that "it was I who saved you, keeping the maddened crowd back by means of my magnetic power! You must never forget that! Never!"[10]

Exhortations revolving around the word "never"—never forget, never again—have been popular in Jewish culture since at least the 1920s, when some Zionists, searching for a battle cry that would encapsulate their belief in Jewish renewal, came across the ancient story of the Jewish warriors atop Masada committing mass suicide rather than surrendering to the Roman legions. In 1926, Yitzhak Lamdan, a poet living in Tel Aviv, composed an epic poem about Jewish suffering and resilience, the highlight of which was the line "Never again should Masada fall!" It became a popular slogan among Zionists worldwide, but as the devastation of the Holocaust became known, "never again" took on a very different meaning. In his 1960 documentary on the rise of Nazism, *Mein Kampf*, the Swedish-Jewish director Erwin Leiser, who fled Germany with his family when he was fifteen, showed the death camp at Auschwitz as the narrator said repeatedly, "It must never happen again—never again." As the genocide's dimensions became better known, another, similar phrase entered the lexicon, "Never forget." Magneto's impassioned speech, then, particularly when coupled with such violent imagery, served to suggest that there were deeper and darker forces at play in the X-Men universe, and that the characters' DNA was subject not only to the mutations that gave them extra powers but also to the epigenetic traumas that guided their actions and shaped their worldview.

Years later, with Lee and Kirby no longer writing and illustrating the series, its new custodian, the Jewish writer Chris Claremont, would explore these ideas, the core of the series' DNA, at great depth. Having spent his childhood on a kibbutz, Claremont saw in Kirby and Lee's characters the potential for telling a seminal story about Jewish life in the aftermath of tragedy. "I was trying to figure out what was the most transfiguring event of our century that would tie in with the super-concept of the X-Men as persecuted outcasts," he said. "It had to be the Holocaust."[11] With that thought in mind, Claremont gave Magneto a backstory of his own: born as Max Eisenhardt to a prosperous German-Jewish family, he was forcibly relocated to the Warsaw Ghetto, where his mother, father, and sister were executed and buried in a mass grave. Thanks to his mutant powers, Max survived, but was soon transported to Auschwitz, where he worked as a member of the *Sonderkommando*, removing the corpses of fellow prisoners from the gas chambers. At the camp, he met and fell in love with a Romani woman named Magda, and the two managed to escape, settling in a small Ukrainian town and giving birth to a daughter, Anya. The villagers, however, soon discovered Magneto's mutant powers, and, terrified, burned down his home with Anya inside. Unable to control his grief and his rage, Magneto let his powers erupt, destroying most of the village. Terrified, Magda left him; she, too, died soon thereafter, but not before giving birth to twins, Pietro and Wanda, who would eventually become Quicksilver and the Scarlet Witch. Magneto, meanwhile, assumed another false identity, Erik Lehnsherr, and traveled to Israel to work with Holocaust survivors in a psychiatric hospital specializing in posttraumatic stress disorder. There, he met another volunteer, Charles Xavier, and the two became friends. Magneto, however, lacked Xavier's compassion, and his ongoing exposure to the victims of Nazi brutalities convinced him that mutants ought to punish humans for their wickedness. He found and stole some buried Nazi gold, which enabled him to start his organization of mutinous mutants, and was soon reunited with his adult children, who helped him in his quest.

"Once I found a point of departure for Magneto," Claremont continued, "all the rest fell into place, because it allowed me to turn him into a tragic figure who wants to save his people. . . . I then had the opportunity . . . to attempt to redeem him . . . to see . . . if he could evolve in the way that Menachem Begin evolved from a guy that the British considered 'Shoot on sight' in 1945 . . . to a statesman who won the Nobel Peace Prize in 1978."[12] In his very first volume at the helm of the X-Men franchise, Claremont had Magneto ponder this theme explicitly. "All my life," the complicated villain says, "I have seen people slaughtered wholesale for no more reason than the deity they worshipped or the color of their skin . . . or the presence in their DNA of an extra, special gene. . . . I cannot change the world but I can . . . and will . . . ensure that my race will never again suffer for [the world's] fear and prejudice."[13]

Claremont was merely picking up where Stan Lee had left off. In one of the earliest X-Men adventures, Professor X and Magneto meet on a mental plane, their rapport clearly well established. "Why??" Magneto roars, "why do you fight us?? For you too are a mutant!!" Unconvinced, Professor X replies, "But I seek to save mankind, not destroy it!"[14]

As intriguing as the premise Lee had set up might have been—two powerful men and two divergent belief systems clashing in a battle for the fate of the world—he hadn't much time to devote to seeing the series through. In 1960, before the arrival of *The Fantastic Four,* Marvel had sold 16.1 million copies of its comics; in 1964, that number rocketed to 27.7 million and slated to continue and grow exponentially.[15] With so many new titles to oversee, and with so many of the characters that were making Lee and his company famous gaining traction with readers, he was increasingly focused on the task that came most naturally, that of establishing Marvel as a publisher with an inimitable voice, the voice of Stan Lee himself.

9

---◆I◆I◆---

Face Front!

WHAT WAS MARVEL ALL ABOUT? In 1965, Stan Lee set out to answer that question, not in a comic book but in another medium he had mastered, a sales pitch. "When fans EYE them, they BUY them!" he boasted of his titles in a brochure meant for comics distributors. That, he went on, had to do with Marvel's "secret formula," which was "bringing in a brand new breed of reader."[1]

Much of that formula had to do with Lee's language. By mid-1965, he had introduced an editorial page of sorts, first called the Merry Marvel Bullpen Page and then Marvel Bull-pen Bulletins, which featured synopses of current titles available in newsstands as well as random bits of gossip about the company's artists and writers. "Face front!" went one typical sample, "everybody's been clamoring for a sample of JACK (King) KIRBY's inking as well as his penciling. So, if you'll remind us next spring, we'll try to get him to pencil and ink a special pin-up page for one of our next year's Annuals! Of course, it'll mean our buying him a brush, but no sacrifice is too great to make for you Marvel madmen!" Readers were then invited to "grab a sheet of your swingin' stationary [sic]" and write to their pal, Smilin' Stan Lee.²

Lee's style, the writer Jonathan Lethem observed, "might be characterized as high hipster—two parts Lord Buckley, one part Austin Powers. Stan Lee was a writer gone Barnum, who'd abandoned new work in favor of rah-rah moguldom. He was Marvel's media liaison and their own biggest in-house fan, a schmoozer. Picture an Orson Welles who'd never bothered to direct films again after *The Lady from Shanghai*, just bullshitted on talk shows, reliving his great moments."³ The quip is amusing, but it misses the point: his expansive fictional universe firmly in place, Lee wasn't merely dining out on past glories, or hustling to get more folks to walk into his circus tent. Instead, he was struggling to connect with a generation that, like him, was trying to make sense of a nation in the throes of some sort of unquiet rebirth.

In December of 1964, furious that the University of California, Berkeley, was refusing him the right of political organization and fundraising, Mario Savio took to the steps of Sproul Hall to urge his fellow students to reconsider their relationship with the university. "If this is a firm," he said to the thousands gathered around him, "and if the Board of Regents are the Board of Directors, and if President Kerr in fact is the manager, then I tell you something—the faculty are a bunch of employees and we're the raw material! . . . We're human beings! And that, that brings me to the second mode of civil disobedience. There's a time when the operation of the machine becomes so odious, makes you so sick at heart that you can't take part! You can't even passively take part! And you've got to put your bodies upon the gears and upon the wheels, upon the levers, upon all the apparatus—and you've got to make it stop!"⁴

Two months later, on February 21, 1965, another impassioned leader was delivering another speech, this one at the Audubon Ballroom in Harlem, when three armed men rushed the stage and fired twenty-one bullets into the chest, arms, legs, and left shoulder of Malcolm X. Two weeks later, hundreds of African-American marchers were viciously clubbed, gassed, and brutalized by Alabama State Troopers as they were marching from Selma to Montgomery. The following day, March 8, thirty-five hundred Marines landed in Vietnam, the first contingent of American combat troops there. By May, thirty thousand people were in attendance as Berkeley's campus was taken over by the largest "teach-in" the university had ever seen. On June 16, fifty thousand demonstrators circled the Pentagon to protest the war; that same day, Robert McNamara announced that an additional twenty-two thousand American soldiers were en route to Vietnam. On August 11, a minor altercation between a motorist and the police unleashed the Watts riots in Los Angeles, which required four thousand members of the California Army National Guard to curb and which resulted in thirty-four deaths and forty million dollars in damages. By November, the Pentagon informed the White House that if the Vietcong were to be subdued, the number of American troops required would have to escalate to 400,000.

In the midst of this violent turmoil, most corners of American officialdom remained oblivious of or hostile to the stirrings of the young. Popular culture, too, for the most part, was doing business as usual. The big winner in the 1965 Academy Awards was *Mary Poppins*, and on TV, the top spot went again to *Bonanza*, a blockbuster since its debut in 1959. And while the British Invasion had already begun in earnest, the radio airwaves were still dominated by sweet, innocuous songs like "This Diamond Ring" by Gary Lewis and the Playboys, a tune so treacly that it made, later that same year, for a perfect cover version by the cartoon characters Alvin and the Chipmunks.

Young Americans, seeking art forms that addressed the turmoil—social, political, emotional, moral—they were experiencing every day, did what they have always done in moments of upheaval and turned to the nation's homegrown art forms. In the 1930s, that meant jazz and Hollywood movies; in the 1960s, attention shifted to rock 'n' roll and comics. The first was libidinal, bacchanalian, cathartic; the second was heady and loose, a sandbox of big but pliable ideas. Both were, in the true tradition of indigenous American art, passionately dedicated to merry theft—of concepts, of backbeats, of aesthetics—and both inhaled, deeply, the fumes of influence, making them ideal instruments for processing anxieties in real time. Like they had been during the Great Depression, America's furies were once again set loose, once again freed from the pews of churches and synagogues and cast into the streets. And again, they demanded to be not only understood but felt as well, a demand that called for art that wasn't afraid of play, that could try on different poses and concepts with little concern for decorum and much attention to that ever-elusive ecstatic truth. If you wanted some benign lesson in how to blow off steam in the approved manner, you could watch Julie Andrews fly off on her umbrella after delivering a mild sentimental jolt to her fictional charges and her real-life viewers alike that did little to upset the social order. But if you wanted to dive into the thrills and difficulties of the mid-to-late sixties, you listened to Jefferson Airplane or to Spider-Man.

Which meant that Lee's job, now that Marvel's sandbox was sufficiently rich, was to make it not only a product but a destination. And to do that, Lee had a three-pronged plan.

First, he resolved to have the comics themselves reflect the realities of American life and embody the convictions Lee shared with the budding counterculture. In 1963, he and Kirby had launched *Sgt. Fury and His Howling Commandos*—the awful name, Lee said years later, was part of a bet with Martin Goodman that a well-written comic could thrive even if burdened with a terrible title—a World War II story featuring one of the most diverse group of characters ever seen in a popular publication. Under the cigar-chomping sergeant's command, the Jewish Izzy Cohen fought side by side with the Italian Dino Manelli and the Irish Dum-Dum Dugan, as well as, more notably, Gabriel Jones, an African-American soldier, and Percival Pinkerton, who Lee—most likely rewriting history, as he sometimes had the knack of doing—later claimed was the first openly gay character in comics. "So there it was," Lee recalled, "a comicbook with a terrible title, starring a platoon made up of various minorities—something for every bigot to dislike."[5] Still, the title did well—Fury would go on to become a central character in the Marvel superhero universe—which convinced Lee that it was time for a superhero who wasn't just another white man.

In July 1966, the Black Panther made his debut in issue number 52 of *The Fantastic Four*, predating by three months the creation of the political party and movement of the same name. He was the alter ego of T'Challa, the ruler of an African nation called Wakanda that was blessed with an alien mineral, Vibranium, that allowed it to develop advanced technologies it kept hidden from the mercenary world outside. The Panther soon befriended the Fantastic Four, joined the Avengers, and registered not only commercial success but also a landmark in American culture, the first black lead of a popular franchise.

Marvel's characters themselves, however, often paled in comparison to Lee himself, whose genius for self-promotion made him something of a cult figure with the young and the restless. To gain a truly committed readership, Lee realized, Marvel couldn't just put out new titles, no matter how socially aware, and hope for the best. It had to state, in the blunt style of the times, that it cared about more than just selling comic books. In 1967, Lee introduced Stan's Soapbox, a new feature published in every Marvel title that allowed him the opportunity to opine, often about the news, and to telegraph to his readers that he wasn't another corporate square.

"Many Keepers of the Faith have demanded that we take a more definitive stand on current problems, such as Viet Nam, civil rights, and the increase in crime, to name a few," went one installment, from September 1967. "We've a hunch that most Marvel madmen pretty well know where we stand on such matters—and we've long believed that our first duty is to entertain, rather than editorialize. Of course, you've probably noticed that it's not too easy to keep our own convictions out of the soul-stirring sagas we toss at you—but, in our own bumbling fashion, we do try. Anyway, since it's YOU who are the true editors of Marveldom, it's time for another impassioned poll! Should we editorialize more—or less—or keep things in the present fouled-up form?"[6] It hardly mattered that Lee never followed up with the poll's results.

Navigating turbulent waters—that same month, September 1967, CBS censored folksinger Pete Seeger's appearance on the Smothers Brothers' variety show, finding it too overtly political—Lee had a distinct talent for assuring his readers he was on their side without ever doing or saying anything that would push him or his company beyond the margins of the generally acceptable. Yet to satisfy his core audience of college kids, he realized that, from time to time, he had no choice but to deliver the loud and fierce sermons that those who had come of age listening to Mario Savio had come to expect.

"Let's lay it right on the line," began a Soapbox column from November 1968. "Bigotry and racism are among the deadliest social ills plaguing the world today. But, unlike a team of costumed supervillains, they can't be halted with a punch in the snoot, or a zap from a ray gun. The only way to destroy them is to expose them—to reveal them for the insidious evils they really are. The bigot is an unreasoning hater—one who hates blindly, fanatically, indiscriminately. If his hang-up is black men, he hates ALL black men. If a redhead once offended him, he hates ALL redheads. If some foreigner beat him to a job, he's down on ALL foreigners. He hates people he's never seen—people he's never known—with equal intensity—with equal venom. Now, we're not trying to say it's unreasonable for one human being to bug another. But, although anyone has the right to dislike another individual, it's totally irrational, patently insane to condemn an entire race—to despise an entire nation—to vilify an entire religion. Sooner or later, we must learn to judge each other on our own merits. Sooner or later, if man is ever to be worthy of his destiny, we must fill our hearts with tolerance. For then, and only then, will we be truly worthy of the concept that man was created in the image of God—a God who calls us ALL—His children. Pax et Justitia, Stan."[7]

But substance was only one path to glory; style was another, every bit as critical to Marvel's success. The Merry Marvel Marching Society was one effective way to let the fans know that the company was committed to hanging loose and having fun: chapters soon popped up on college campuses all over the country, and demand was so high that Flo Steinberg, Lee's assistant, had to come in on weekends to make sure every fan received his or her membership kit. "We had to write down everybody's name and make labels for each one, and pull out all these hundreds of dollar bills," she later remembered. "We were throwing them at each other there were so many!"[8] Soon fans started calling Marvel's offices, eager to chat with the writers and editors Lee had made so accessible by giving them nicknames and personas, and soon after that college students occasionally made it up to Marvel's offices on 625 Madison Avenue, hoping to bump into their pals, King Kirby or Stan the Man.

Lee, however, hardly waited for his fans to come to him, and began touring college campuses nationwide. At first, he was surprised by the attention, unsure of how a forty-four-year-old

writer might go about addressing kids who were considerably
younger and better educated than he. One recording of an early
appearance in Princeton reveals an almost bashful Lee feeling
his way through a room full of wordy and nerdy admirers. After
delivering a short and uncharacteristically awkward introduction, Lee opened the floor to questions, and, immediately, one
young man jumped up with a query about Thor and the gods
who battled each other in the comic.

"Something's been bothering me for a while," the fan said,
"and that is, if Odin is the lord of the universe, how does he
tolerate the existence of Zeus? How can you have these gods
ruling the universe at the same time?" Lee didn't have to think
for long. "Sometimes these question and answer periods go on
too long," he replied, the joke only barely masking his discom-
fort with suddenly spending his days not at the Marvel bullpen,
coming up with plots for dozens of comic books a month, but
behind a podium in a lecture hall, responding to queries suggesting that his creations were canonical.[9]

Lee's apprehension, however, was short-lived. His sessions
with student fans, he realized, provided an opportunity to do
market research, and he soon developed a routine that involved
about twenty minutes of friendly banter about the inner work-
ings of Marvel followed by a Q and A of about an hour that
enabled Lee to hear what his readers had in mind and then rush
back to the office and work their ideas into plot points. A number of these appearances were documented by college newspapers, which led arbiters of taste on a grander scale to pay attention as well: "Marvel Comics," wrote a reporter for the *Village
Voice*, then still the paragon of downtown cool and literary so-
phistication, "are the first comic books in history in which a
post-adolescent escapist can get involved. For Marvel Comics
are the first comic books to evoke, even metaphorically, the Real
World."[10] And the Unreal World, too: encouraged by Harold
Pinter to stage his experimental play, a sexually charged dia-

logue between Jean Harlow and Billy the Kid, the poet Michael McClure had the starlet tease the cowboy in the play's very first lines with an existential question. "Before you can pry any secrets from me," she purrs, "you must find the real me. Which one will you pursue?"[11] Harlow repeats the line again and again throughout the play, even though few of its viewers at the time probably realized that McClure had borrowed the refrain from Lee and Ditko's Dr. Strange.

Of course, not everyone was adoring: talk show host Dick Cavett, visibly uncomfortable with giving a comic book writer the spotlight reserved for men like Gore Vidal or James Baldwin, tried his best to remain polite when he had Lee on his show in 1968, but the comic Pat McCormick, another guest, was less reserved. As soon as Lee finished answering a question about the Marvel heroes college kids loved most, which involved telling McCormick and Cavett—neither of whom was very familiar with Lee or his work—about the Hulk, the corpulent comedian giggled. "Is that the one that Bertrand Russell writes?" McCormick quipped, and Lee, smiling tensely, replied, "Well, it's very complimentary of you." Further banter ensued, most of it at Lee's expense, but the comics creator, like one of his afflicted superheroes, returned to triumph over his adversaries in the final act. "We are very interested in the youth," he said, letting his earnestness shine against McCormick's glib patter. "We are very aware, or try to be aware, of what's happening. We're trying to do whatever we can to make things a little better. I think the more power we can get through these stories, and the more moral the tone of these books we can make, the better it is for everybody." Visibly moved, Cavett asked a few more questions, and then inquired whether McCormick had ever seen a copy of *The Mighty Thor*. "It has two-syllable words," Lee jumped in, beaming at the comedian, "so you might have a little difficulty." The audience gasped, Lee smiled victoriously, and those watching at home were left without a doubt as to who was the coolest cat on the screen.[12]

Observing Lee's transformation from the affable guy who played his ocarina around the office while dreaming up stories about men in tights to a sought-after icon of the counterculture, more than a few of his colleagues at Martin Goodman's publishing empire raised their eyebrows. They raised them even higher when, one day in 1965, Flo Steinberg rang Lee on the office phone to inform him that some men had come to see him. "I don't know their names," she said, "but the head one seems to be Felony." Lee went over to the office lobby to greet his guests, who turned out to be Federico Fellini and his entourage, in town to promote *Juliet of the Spirits*. Alain Resnais was a fan as well, and a note to Lee led first to a correspondence and eventually to a friendship that culminated in the director of *Hiroshima Mon Amour* coming to America and staying in Lee's guesthouse on Long Island while collaborating on a script for a monster movie about the dangers of pollution.[13] But while some in the office—like Mario Puzo, a few years away from publishing *The Godfather* and earning a living writing for Goodman's men's magazines—were amused by Lee's unlikely rise to stardom, others were incensed, and none more so than Goodman himself.

"As time went by," Lee wrote in his memoir, "I began to notice a change in him. For some inexplicable reason, the more our sales increased, the colder his attitude toward me seemed to become. At first I thought I was imagining it, but then he'd start needling me about things, telling me in gloating tones that if he woke up one morning and decided to raise the cover price of our magazines by a few pennies, the company would make more money by that one decision than by all the work I could do in a year. He also let me know in no uncertain terms that he paid the editors and writers of his movie magazines and so-called sophisticated men's magazines far more than he paid his comicbook staff, because he was prouder to be the publisher of the 'slicks' since they were on a higher cultural plateau than his lowly comicbooks. In fact, I started to fear that I was becoming paranoid, because I began to think he almost resented the success of our comics line. I felt it wouldn't displease him to see sales slip and have my confidence taken down a peg. To put it bluntly, I think he was beginning to perceive me as more of a competitor than an employee."[14]

Such resentment was shared by several other people in Lee's orbit. The Marvel Method—which allowed Lee to deliver general plotlines and count on his artists to fill in not only the art but also crucial components of the story before Lee himself jumped back in to write the script—was vital to making sure he could work on several titles simultaneously, but it also left a number of people in the Marvel office feeling as if Lee was taking credit for what was truly a collaboration of equals. Jack Kirby was particularly frustrated. He was just as much the creator of the X-Men and the Fantastic Four and the Avengers, yet he was still being paid by the page and enjoyed neither long-term financial security nor the kind of acclaim with which Lee was being showered daily. For the most part, he just grumbled on and sat back down at his desk in the basement studio he lovingly called the Dungeon. But on one occasion, Lee's fame left him reeling.

It was late in 1965, and Nat Freedland, a reporter for the *New York Herald Tribune*, came to Marvel's offices to profile its most celebrated employee. Lee was charming and self-deprecating, striking a besotted Freedland as an "ultra-Madison Avenue, rangy lookalike of Rex Harrison." Permitted to sit in on a story meeting, Freedland depicted some of the back-and-forth between Lee and Kirby, giving his readers a taste of the Marvel Method in action but making sure they knew who the real star was. If Lee was the confident charmer, Freedland continued, Kirby was "a middle-aged man with baggy eyes and a baggy Robert Hall-ish suit. He is sucking a huge green cigar and if you stood next to him on the subway you would peg him for the assistant foreman in a girdle factory."[15]

The piece was published early on the morning of January 9, 1966. A few hours later, Lee's phone rang. It was Roz Kirby, Jack's wife. "She was almost hysterical," Lee recalled, "and she shouted, 'How could you do this? How could you have done this to Jack?'"[16] Lee apologized and promised he'd do his best to make sure people realized Jack was his partner, not some schlub who slumped around the office and obediently executed Lee's radiant vision. Still, the incident left Kirby feeling wounded, and from the depths of his frustration emerged perhaps the greatest work he and Lee had ever created, a story about a soulful alien and the angry god who tests him, a morality tale so profoundly moving it remains one of the greatest works in comic book history, as well as, sadly, one of the last ones Stan Lee and Jack Kirby would ever produce together.

10

My Own Power Has Never Been Fully Tested!

Like so many of Marvel's superheroes, the Silver Surfer had a troubled birth.

The iconic story of how he came to be, almost certainly false but passed from one generation of fans to another like a bit of sacred lore, has Lee delivering Kirby a note with a four-word plot point for the next adventure of the Fantastic Four: "Have them fight God." Neither man ever confirmed the account. In fact, Kirby, speaking to his biographer years later, cited a much more earthly form of inspiration: he was reading a newspaper article on corporate raiders who took over successful companies, emptied them of their assets, and moved on to their next scheme. It struck a nerve. Ever the street-fighting tough kid, Kirby sensed Martin Goodman's strange resentment of Marvel's success, and he'd heard rumors that the boss was talking to all sorts of people about possibly selling the company. If that happened, Kirby knew, he would stand to lose the most. He had no pension, no long-term contract, no guarantees of future employment, and none of Lee's public relations sheen. In that ominous mood, he sat down to riff on whatever it was that Lee had handed him by way of plot for issue number 48 of *The Fantastic Four.* And the creature that emerged from his burdened mind was Galactus.

A massive being in a horned helmet, his outfit some impossible continuum of Greek dress and high-tech space suit, Galactus wore a large G on his chest, a literal indication that he was the closest thing comicdom had ever seen to God. In pure biblical fashion, Kirby and Lee launch the story with the sky above New York City suddenly consumed by flames. The Fantastic Four, returning from a daunting mission in space, leap to action, but they have little luck dealing with either the fiery skies or with the terrified population in the streets below. Soon, the fire gives way to another plaguelike scene, as the skyline is covered with floating rocks. Unable to figure out the cause of all this pandemonium, Mr. Fantastic grows distraught; he stops shaving or eating, causing Sue Storm to grow increasingly worried about his health. Far from the usual comic book rhythm of one action sequence igniting another, Lee and Kirby build an ominous atmosphere in just a few pages, preparing their heroes—and their readers—for the worst.

The worst soon arrives, taking the form of a supernatural being called the Watcher. A benevolent cosmic titan, he is a member of an ancient race tasked with spreading wisdom across the galaxy and tormented by the destruction of their own home planet, which had condemned the Watchers to deep space exile. This creature, a thinly veiled metaphor for Jewish history, emerges to confess that it was he who blanketed the sky with fire and rocks, in an effort, he says, to conceal the planet from Galactus. The omnipotent alien, the Watcher explains, feeds on the energy of planets, leaving them dry and lifeless. And he had now discovered Earth. Or, rather, his herald had.

That would be the Silver Surfer, perhaps Kirby's greatest creation. Having discussed the plot with the artist, Lee was surprised, looking at Kirby's pages, to see a metallic being tearing through the cosmos on a surfboard. It was one thing for Kirby to fill in a plot point here or there—that, in fact, was what the Marvel Method was all about—but creating an entirely new character was unprecedented. "I'm looking through the drawings," Lee recalled, "I see this nut on a surfboard flying through the air. And I thought, 'Jack, this time you've gone too far.'"[1]

But if Lee the editor was skeptical, Lee the writer was intrigued. Introducing the Surfer, Kirby used his signature Kirby Crackle to greater effect than ever before, having his new creature slide down pulsating paths of blue and red and green. And his note to Lee made perfect sense: if Galactus was to be a god, Kirby reasoned, he should have an avenging angel in his employ, some celestial being doing his darkest biddings.

With this theological mindset, Lee and Kirby set out to plot the rest of the story. Once the Surfer glides onto Earth, he summons his master, who arrives in a terrifying and majestic full-page photo collage, the first time Kirby had used the technique in a comic book. In it, New York's skyline is a black broth illuminated by bursts of bright yellow and shadowed by a massive spaceship glowing in an ethereal blue. It's the sort of visual that would've fit right into *2001: A Space Odyssey*, which Stanley Kubrick would release two years later, in 1968. But even for such an early entry into the modern science fiction canon, the image left no doubt that the being in the blue spacecraft was a departure from everything that had appeared in the pages of a comic book before him.

This sense of doom generated by the arrival of a menacing alien is only amplified in the next comic, in which the Four set out to fight Galactus. Long an expert on all-powerful villains, Lee knew that one of the biggest challenges every comic writer faced involved making the bad guys seem mighty enough to pose a threat but not too mighty as to appear invincible. The superheroes, after all, must always prevail, but how might they prevail against an omnipotent creature like Galactus? The question fascinated Lee, and, to explore it, he applied an ancient dramatic device, one lifted directly from the book of Numbers.

There, Moses dispatches twelve spies to tour the land of Canaan, the promised haven the Israelites hope to enter. Ten of the spies, however, return trembling with fear, reporting that the Promised Land does not flow with milk and honey but swarms with hostile giants. "And we were in our own sight as grasshoppers," they say, "and so we were in their sight."[2] Their sin, we learn from the numerous rabbinic interpretations of the story, wasn't just that they failed to see the land's potential and focused instead on its shortcomings, but that they allowed their own notion of self-worth to be thwarted, imagining that their powerful enemies saw them as nothing more than pesky insects and coming to see themselves the same way. Standing before Galactus, the Fantastic Four commit the same sin: in several full-page panels, we see the Four literally dwarfed by the imperious alien, often delivering desperate monologues of self-doubt. "See how he ignores us . . . as though we're of no consequence!"[3] Mr. Fantastic yelps, gazing at Galactus's massive arms. A few panels later, he lands on the biblical grasshopper imagery: "Can't you tell?" he complains as Galactus drops a small bomb that has the Four scrambling for safety. "He's treating us like some sort of bothersome gnats! It's a type of cosmic insect repellent!"[4]

This uncharacteristic loss of faith indicates that the struggle the Four must win will be metaphysical in nature. They realize it, too, which is why they retreat to their headquarters in the Baxter Building and engage in quiet contemplation. Mr. Fantastic, for example, enjoys a leisurely shave, explaining to the others that there's "no harm in tidying up while we're thinking."[5] But while the Four linger, the book's real hero, the Surfer, is about to have an awakening of his own. Clobbered by the

Thing, he is tossed to a nearby roof where, stunned and wounded, he finds an open skylight and slips listlessly into the room below. It's the studio of Alicia Masters, the blind sculptor who is also the Thing's love interest, and even though she can't see the Surfer falling in, she senses his arrival and rushes to his side. In a trope lifted from the classic monster movies of the 1930s—the sensitive woman who is the only one who dares befriend the creature everyone else fears and loathes—Masters nurses the Surfer back to health. And when he finally speaks, the extent of Lee's infatuation with the character becomes apparent.

Rather than crack wise like everyone else in the Marvel universe, spitting out puns and catchphrases layered with the occasional meaningful moment of introspection, the Surfer speaks in a stentorian biblical cadence that matches his otherworldly stare. When Masters tells him she does not understand who he is, he glares into the distance and replies, "What does it matter? Understanding cannot alter the ways of destiny!"[6] With that, the stage is set for the strangest and most significant battle a Marvel character had ever waged, the attempt by a disabled woman with no powers other than reason and compassion to convince a heartless and powerful alien that humanity is worth saving.

The Four, meanwhile, endure their own spiritual turbulence nearby: the only way to stop Galactus, the Watcher informs them, is to obtain a tool called the Ultimate Nullifier, a MacGuffin if there ever was one. The Nullifier, naturally, is hidden in the farthest recesses of the cosmos, which means that the Human Torch would have to risk annihilation to retrieve it before Galactus drains Earth of life. "You are traveling back . . . Far, far back . . . Into the center of infinity!" the Watcher informs the Torch as the teenager's tortured face, his mouth frozen in a silent scream, disappears into orbs of white and pink and yellow. "You have already ceased to exist in your own time continuum . . . The distance you are traveling is so great that your language holds no words which can describe it!"[7] Kirby's illustrations capture the infinity and emptiness of space so well that readers are left wondering whether the Torch will ever be able to find his way through all this nothingness, and even if he does, to return safely to his planet and to his consciousness, unharmed by the toll the journey has taken on his mind. There's nothing else onerous about his voyage, no space monsters to battle or asteroids to dodge, just the maddening strain of a human being forced to contemplate the whole of creation.

As Johnny Storm flames on in outer space, Alicia Masters is in her apartment, banging her fists against the Surfer's silver chest. "You intend to destroy the Earth!" she howls, and the Surfer, placid as always, disagrees. "Destroy is merely a word!" he responds. "We simply change things! We change elements into energy . . . The energy which sustains Galactus! For it is only he that matters!" The statement makes Masters furious. "No!" she screams, "No! We all matter! Every living being . . . Every bird and beast . . . This is our world! Ours!"[8]

The line recalls a famous Talmudic exchange that has come to serve as shorthand for a key precept of Jewish theology, namely the complicated nature of the relationship between God and Man. In it, a host of rabbis are debating the ritual purity of a particular type of oven. All are in agreement that the oven is impure, except for Rabbi Eliezer, who brings the full weight of his scholarship into the argument. When his fellow rabbis are still not convinced, Eliezer, frustrated, calls for a miracle. "If the *halakha* [Jewish law] is in accordance with my opinion," he thunders, "this carob tree will prove it." And just like that, the tree is uprooted, tiptoes across 150 feet, and replants itself in the ground. Eliezer gloats, but his colleagues are unmoved. "One does not cite *halakhic* proof from the carob tree," they say. Eliezer grows angrier. "If the *halakha* is in accordance with my opinion," he says, "this stream will prove it," at which moment the water in the stream begins flowing backward. "One," the other rabbis retort, "does not cite *halakhic* proof from a stream." This goes on for a while, until Eliezer calls on the ultimate adjudicator. "If the *halakha* is in accordance with my opinion," he declares, "heaven will prove it." No sooner is he done talking than a divine voice is heard in the study hall. "Why are you differing with Rabbi Eliezer," it says, "as the *halakha* is in accordance with his opinion in every place that he expresses an opinion?" But the debate is far from over. Leaping to his feet, Rabbi Yehoshua says "It is not in heaven," meaning that once the Torah was given by God to human beings, it's up to us on Earth, not Him in heaven, to decide what things truly mean. The story ends with an anecdote, taking place years later, in which Rabbi Natan meets the prophet Elijah and asks him what God thought of the whole feisty exchange. "Elijah," the Talmud concludes, "said to him: The Holy One, Blessed be He, smiled and said: My children have triumphed over Me; My children have triumphed over Me."[9]

The Surfer feels the same way. "Never have I heard such words," he tells Masters, "sensed such courage . . . or known this strange feeling . . . this new emotion!"[10] That strange feeling is the awakening of the Surfer's moral sensibility, a previously unfelt inclination to stand up for the innocent creatures his celestial master destroys without as much as a second thought. Leaping on his board, the Surfer resolves to do the unthinkable and stand up to Galactus. "My own power," he says as he rushes to the showdown, "has never been fully tested!"[11]

He arrives just in time. The Four, watching helplessly as Galactus makes the final preparation for Armageddon, teeter on the verge of despair. "He's so big," sighs Sue Storm, "so powerful . . . With weapons we've never heard of! What chance can we have?" Not sounding particularly convinced of his own words, Mr. Fantastic says, "There's always a chance, darling . . . So long as we're alive!" And the Thing, happy as always to take a swipe at his colleague, asks, "Yeah? How much longer'll that be?"[12]

Fans seeking an answer to the question had to wait until the next issue, titled "The Startling Saga of the Silver Surfer" and celebrated on its first page with a message from Lee that declared the book "peerless pageantry, at the peak of proud perfection!"[13] What followed, however, betrayed little of Marvel's excited, alliterative style. "Master!" the Surfer pleads with Galactus on the very first page, "For the first time I realize the dreadful enormity of what you plan to do! You must not tamper with other worlds! You cannot destroy the entire human race!"[14]

Galactus scoffs at his servant's newfound sensibility, telling him that Earth is no more than an anthill. Unmoved, the Surfer makes another plea for mercy, and when Galactus refuses to listen, he confronts his master directly. "I too am a creature of the cosmos!!" he states. "I too can unleash forces which, once released, can never again be controlled!"[15] To prove his point, he strikes Galactus with his potent energy bolts, and the deity, stunned, accuses the Surfer of betrayal. "Betray you??" the Surfer replies, "Never! But in truth, I should betray myself if I did not fight to prevent the annihilation of a people! For here . . . On this lonely little world . . . I have found what men call . . . conscience!"[16]

It's a moving story of the ultimate test anyone can face, the courage to stand up to one's heavenly lord. It's also lifted, with few alterations, from the book of Genesis. There, in chapter 18, God tells Abraham that he is about to strike Sodom and Gomorrah and punish the wicked men there for their sins. Astonishingly, Abraham objects. He has never met the condemned, but he has developed what men call a conscience, and he isn't about to sit idly by as God smites his children. Like the Surfer, Abraham had served his God faithfully; like the Surfer, too, he has left his home and wandered wherever God told him to go; and like the Surfer, he is now fighting for the right of perfect strangers to live.

"And Abraham drew near, and said, Wilt thou also destroy

the righteous with the wicked? Peradventure there be fifty righteous within the city: wilt thou also destroy and not spare the place for the fifty righteous that are therein?"[17] God, surprised, agrees to spare the town if fifty righteous men can be found, but, for Abraham, the negotiation is only beginning: with little consideration for his own interests, he convinces God to spare Sodom and Gomorrah for forty righteous men, then thirty, twenty, and finally, ten. Sadly, the accursed cities can't produce even a handful of innocents, and are soon destroyed. But Abraham has transformed himself regardless, entering what the philosopher Susan Neiman calls "resolute universalism." The Abraham "who risked God's wrath to argue for the lives of unknown innocents," she writes, "is the kind of man who would face down injustice anywhere."[18] No longer seeing his fellow human beings as mere abstractions, he is willing to interfere in their lives just as God does, fighting on their behalf, realizing, in Kierkegaard's famous phrase, that religious reason is higher than mere ethical reason precisely because it calls on such acts of radical empathy without which true justice would be difficult if not impossible.[19]

Like God, Galactus is impressed with his servant's noble transformation. Unlike God, he reasons that disobedience must nonetheless be punished. After the Human Torch returns with the Nullifier and forces him to retreat, Galactus robs the Surfer of his ability to travel the Cosmos, condemning him to remain on Earth for all eternity. "At last I perceive the glint of glory within the race of man!" Galactus says as he departs amid a red storm of cosmic currents. "Be ever-worthy of that glory, humans . . . Be ever mindful of your promise of greatness! For it shall one day lift you beyond the stars or bury you within the ruins of war!! The choice is yours!!"[20]

Humans being humans, they choose poorly: as the book ends, Lee and Kirby give readers two more pages of anticlimax, beginning with the Thing feeling jealous of Alicia Masters's affection for the Surfer and ending with J. Jonah Jameson, Spider-Man's tormenter, arguing on the front page of his *Daily Bugle* that Galactus was nothing but a hoax perpetrated by the Four in a desperate bid for attention.

Despite the grim ending, or maybe because of it, readers immediately understood that the Galactus Trilogy, as it came to be called, was a departure, even for Lee and Marvel. It was one thing to revive the comic book form by featuring fun superheroes who did battle with a parade of predators while occasionally touching on deep ethical questions and alluding to the Bible and Jewish theology. It was another thing altogether to deliver a three-book story arc that dealt directly with the crisis of faith, the limits of reason, and the bloom of morality. Eager to make sense of the story, many wrote Marvel to suggest that the whole tale was somehow an allegory for the war in Vietnam, a warning against destruction, and a call to Americans to find their own conviction and emulate the Surfer's courage. In his signature style, Lee gently mocked these fan theories. "Two'll getcha ten that our next mail contains a whole caboodle of letters from equally imaginative fans who are utterly convinced that Galactus represented Robert McNamara, while the Silver Surfer was Wayne Morse—with Alicia symbolizing Lady Bird!"[21]

Lee's joke, however, masked his growing obsession with the figure he now called the Sentinel of the Spaceways. More than any other Marvel character, the Surfer allowed him to fulfill his boyhood fantasy of writing great literary works that explored humanity in all its complications. Over the course of the next two years, the Surfer made repeated appearances in various Marvel comic books, and even if none approached the grandeur of his debut, Lee still found the Surfer to be the perfect vehicle for his increasingly bold theological explorations. In *The Fantastic Four* number 72, for example, the Surfer resolves to make himself the enemy of mankind in a desperate bid to unite it and keep it from destroying itself with needless wars and festering extremism. Again, the Four greet the news with despair. "But what . . . can he do . . . against the all-powerful Silver Surfer?" Sue Storm asks when Mr. Fantastic sets out to battle the alien, but the Watcher, on hand again to help mankind survive, sneers at her folly. "All-powerful?" he asks. "There is only one who deserves that name! And his only weapon is love!"[22]

Jack Kirby, too, had high hopes for the Surfer, and was at work on a new story featuring his origins when he learned, late in 1967, that Lee was giving the character his own comic book series. Instead of Kirby, he had chosen another artist, John Buscema, to illustrate it, and the first issue was already en route to the printer. Even more stinging for the artist, rather than honor Kirby's idea and make the Surfer a being of pure energy—that, Kirby reasoned, would explain why the Surfer was so ignorant of basic human concepts like love, fear, and anger—Lee reimagined the Surfer as having once been a humanlike figure who had teamed up with Galactus and sacrificed his human form to save the woman he loved.

Seeing his creation taken away from him left Kirby feeling more insecure than ever before. There was no point, he knew, in taking it up with Lee, who argued, whenever Kirby came complaining, that both of them were merely Marvel employees and that there was nothing Lee could do to make sure the company awarded Kirby the respect and compensation he deserved. Bitter, Kirby resolved to keep his duties to a minimum, keeping to himself any further characters or story lines until he could come to a satisfactory arrangement with Martin Goodman. There would be, his wife, Roz Kirby, put it, "no more Silver Surfers until he gets a better deal."[23]

If Lee noticed the deepening of his partner's frustration, he said or did little to address it. Instead, he was busy thinking about the future. Early in 1966, *Batman*, a half-hour series based on DC Comics' famous character, debuted on ABC, quickly becoming the most popular show on TV. To Lee, struggling to make Marvel bigger than its main competitor in comics, that was bad news. Even worse was the fact that the show's writer, Lorenzo Semple Jr., had reimagined the Caped Crusader and his sidekick Robin as a pair of self-aware superheroes, giving the show a humorous, tongue-in-cheek tone that fit right in with the sensibility Lee had toiled to create at Marvel for half a decade. Semple even applied the superhero crossover plot device, a Marvel staple, having Van Williams and Bruce Lee make guest appearances as the Green Hornet and Kato to promote their own superhero TV show. When *TV Guide* profiled Williams in late 1966, noting his off-camera success as a savvy investor, the article's subheading referred to him as "your friendly neighborhood tycoon," a play on the phrase Stan Lee had popularized to describe his most famous creation, Spider-Man.[24] To add insult to injury, an animated series based on Lee's characters, saddled with the flightless title *The Marvel Super Heroes*, was released in 1966 as well. It was never continued past its initial sixty-five-episode run, and was largely considered too silly to take seriously.

It was the worst thing that could happen to a master craftsman of public image. Lee had toiled for years to define and refine the Marvel sensibility, building it into a brand long before marketing mavens wised up to the term and its specifications. And now here were his competitors co-opting his ideas, and here was the press using his language as shorthand for all comics everywhere. Not being in a position of real corporate power— he was adequately compensated for his work, but owned none of the rights to his characters—there was little he could do to navigate Marvel to more promising waters. And Goodman, he thought, was far from the world's optimal boss: a salesman who had struck it big in a very different era, an insecure businessman begrudging Lee his renown, there was no telling what steps, if any, he would take to compete with DC, and what these steps would mean for Lee himself. Ever the boy shaped by the pain of the Great Depression and the fear of unemployment, Lee resolved to double down on the only Marvel character over which he had complete control: Stan Lee.

11

This Long-Awaited Leap

THE NEW COMIC BOOK they will soon hold in their hands, Stan Lee informed his readers in his Soapbox editorial in May of 1968, will be "a magazine as different from the ordinary comic as a guided missile is different from a spitball!" After a bit of playful teasing—the magazine, Lee elaborated, would feature Spider-Man and cost a whopping thirty-five cents, nearly three times the price of an ordinary comic book—Lee turned serious, vowing that his latest work would be his greatest yet. "All of comicdom has been demanding this giant step forward," he wrote, "this long-awaited leap to the next plateau of literary greatness."[1]

When the book was released in July, under the title *The Spectacular Spider-Man*, it featured a cover painted in acrylic, giving it a more adult look. To further the book's gravitas, it was printed in black-and-white, a move Lee hoped would finally help Marvel cross over from kids and college students to the general adult reading public.

It didn't. The new Spider-Man was anything but spectacularly received, and Lee, long accustomed to success, licked his wounds by focusing all of his attention on those readers who loved him best and dialing up the frequency and the intensity of his campus visits. Instead of dropping in, speaking for a short while, and heading back to his hotel, Lee now spent hours, even days, hanging out with his young fans. Robert Lawrence, the animated show's producer, accompanied Lee on some of these visits. "The kids were unbelievable," he recalled. "I think we spent three days at Chapel Hill with them. They'd stay up all night drinking beers, speaking to Stan Lee."[2] Fittingly, then, in its annual college issue, *Esquire* devoted six pages, in full color, to Marvel's characters, reporting that the company had "sold 50,000 printed t-shirts and 30,000 sweat shirts, and it has run out of adult sizes of both."[3]

Ever mindful of appearances, Lee took to wearing a toupee to cover his receding hairline, and grew a beard that made him look less like a middle-aged writer and more like some elder statesman of cool the young things on the quad could respect. Not that respect was the only currency of cool: eager to show their hip readers that they were not above a bit of self-parody, Lee and Kirby collaborated on a new title called *Not Brand Echh*, which poked fun at their iconic heroes while appealing to some of the average collegiate's favorite things. The debut issue, for example, featured the Silver Burper offering a bong-like device to the Thung and urging him to inhale, while back in the Bopster Building Weed Wichards was preparing to fight his archnemesis, Doctor Bloom, and the Human Scorch exclaimed "Hey—watch it, Weed! That stuff burns!"[4] Also, with Marvel's suits discontinuing the Merry Marvel Marching Society—Martin Goodman had decided that it contributed little to the company's bottom line and therefore had to be eliminated—

Lee came up with another gimmick to engage the readers, sending out a series of No-Prizes, stamped envelopes containing absolutely nothing.

But just as Lee was eagerly connecting with the teen spirit, two cataclysmic events foiled his plans for the future. The first occurred thousands of miles away: with the Tet offensive catching American forces by surprise and claiming tens of thousands of lives, the war in Vietnam, already a highly divisive issue, spiraled into a full-blown crisis. On February 23, 1968, the U.S. Selective Service System issued a new draft call for forty-eight thousand men, the second-highest requisition in the war's short and bloody history. Five days later, Secretary of Defense Robert S. McNamara resigned. In early March, Walter Cronkite, the nation's most trusted man, announced on the air that he believed only peace talks could end the stalemate in Vietnam, and on March 31 President Lyndon B. Johnson shocked the nation when he announced that he would not seek reelection. Martin Luther King Jr. was assassinated in April, Robert F. Kennedy in June. The country's political system was in turmoil, and increasingly, young Americans expected their artists to address the chaos that roared all around them.

Lee wasn't ready to do anything of the sort. He was a moderate liberal who shared most of his young readers' frustrations and applauded their commitment to social justice, but he was, above all else, a canny promoter who knew that nothing could be more deadly to a product than taking sides in a heated controversy. "Our thinking," he told a fan who confronted him during one Q and A panel with an accusation that Marvel was insufficiently political, "is that the pages of our comics magazines may not be the right place for getting too heavy handed with social messages of any sort. We may be wrong. Maybe we should come out more forcibly and maybe we will."[5] Marvel soon did, or, at least, tried to: a few months later, *The Amazing Spider-Man* number 68, which hit newsstands as the tumultuous year was drawing to its end, featured the web-slinger zooming above a horde of angry students carrying signs, in a story titled "Crisis on Campus!"

After a prolonged and almost laughable demonstration of force by the Kingpin, one of Spider-Man's lesser enemies, who announces his intention to steal an all-powerful ancient tablet, the story shifts to Peter Parker arriving at Empire State University, where he's a student, only to stumble upon a big demonstration. He asks its leader, an African-American student named Josh, what it's all about, and is treated to a rude reply. "Look, whitey," Josh says, "how much do you haveta know?" Josh then tersely explains that he and his friends demand that the university turn one of its halls into housing for low-income students, and, again, Peter is reluctant, asking what the dean thinks of the demand. "We ain't buyin' what he says!" Josh declares. "From now on, we do the talking!" This brazen style of conversation turns Parker off; "Anyone can paint a sign, mister!" he says. "That doesn't make you right!" But just as Parker sulks about the situation, Josh and his friends decide to take over the hall, just as real-life students had done at Columbia University a few months earlier. The hall, however, is showcasing an exhibit of the very tablet the Kingpin wants to steal. The officers guarding it draw their weapons at the students, and Parker, watching from the sidelines, grows distraught. "In a spot like this," he says, "anything can happen. But what can I . . . what can anybody . . . do about it now? At a time like this . . . even Spidey would be helpless!"

When the Kingpin shows up, however, Parker has no choice but to change into his Spider-Man costume and fight the villain, who hopes to steal the tablet and blame it on the young protestors. The radicals, on their end, spot Spider-Man and are sure that he, like the Kingpin, is their enemy, and a melee ensues that ends with the Kingpin fleeing with the tablet, the protestors arrested, and Spider-Man ending his adventure not with a bang but with a whimper.[6] The unfortunate story arc ended two issues later, with the dean reconciling with the protestors, telling them he was working behind the scenes to further their cause with the school's board, and apologizing for not being a better listener.

The story line stands as a validation of Lee's insistence that comic books should focus on stories, not sermons. Its juxtapositions—between the Kingpin's outlandish and the students' all-too-real demands, between Spider-Man's banter and the protestors' angrily righteous language—are jarring, making for a comic book that is neither entertaining nor edifying. Going political, Lee was learning, would mean compromising Marvel's style, and trading his timeless explorations of morality for the far shallower and more furious surface of the here-and-now.

If the nation was in turmoil, however, so was Marvel itself. In June, Martin Goodman was approached by a mergers and acquisitions magnate named Martin Ackerman, with an offer he couldn't refuse. Ackerman had made his fortune buying distinct businesses—cigar shops, pharmacies, film labs—and pasting them together under one roof, which he named the Perfect Film and Chemical Corporation. Earlier in 1968, he had bought Curtis Publishing, the venerable home of *Ladies' Home Journal* and *The Saturday Evening Post*, where Norman Rockwell had spent decades crafting a vision of the best angels of America's nature. Ackerman wasn't quite so idealistic: "I'm Marty Ackerman," he told his new employees the first time he met them. "I'm 36 years old and I am very rich. I hope to make the Curtis Company rich again."[7] In his office, a fancy townhouse on the Upper East Side, he had an oil portrait of himself clutching the *Wall Street Journal*. Goodman was impressed, and agreed to sell his company for fifteen million dollars in cash and some Perfect Film stock, while remaining on board as publisher. The only condition, Ackerman said, was that Stan Lee must stay with the company.

"I thought the notion was pretty damn flattering," Lee recalled in his autobiography. "One of my closest friends, who also happened to be a brilliant businessman, was Marshall Finck, chairman of the board of a major company. He told me I was in a great position since my being under contract was 'of the essence' for the sale being made. Marshall said I could ask Martin for almost anything and he would have to give it to me." But Lee was never one for haggling with the boss. "Do you think I'd insult him by saying, 'What are you going to give me?'" he asked Finck. "I know he'll be fair," he continued. "I'm not some money-grubbing ingrate who's gonna take advantage of the situation." Ever loyal to Goodman, Lee never considered speaking to Ackerman directly.

Finck, Lee recalled, "just shook his head sadly, sighed, and walked away." He knew what he was talking about. The next evening, Lee and his wife had dinner with the Goodmans, and Marvel's longtime boss promised Lee "some valuable warrants" if he stayed with the company. Lee agreed. But no warrants, valuable or otherwise, ever exchanged hands.[8]

Before Lee could get used to the new reality at Marvel, it changed once again, with Ackerman leaving his own company and being replaced by Sheldon Feinberg, the former CFO of Revlon. Born poor and made tough by a life in business, Feinberg believed a boss governed best by intimidating his underlings, and charged into the Marvel offices demanding efficiency, obedience, and discipline, not exactly the conditions that best serve creative souls. Unfortunately, it was in the midst of this transition that Jack Kirby's contract with Marvel expired. Asked by Lee to pinch-hit on *The Silver Surfer*—still a sore spot with Kirby—he waited for his lawyer to negotiate a new contract he hoped would grant him the recognition and security that had long eluded him. But Feinberg cared little for artists, and, unlike Stan Lee, he hadn't heard of Jack Kirby, assuming the King of Comics was just another grumpy artist with an inflated ego. When the new contract arrived, Kirby was incensed to discover that it gave him even less favorable terms than before. After decades at Marvel and years of flirting with DC Comics, he called that company's boss, Carmine Infantino, and signed a three-year deal with Marvel's biggest competitor.

Kirby had assumed Lee would help him talk some sense into Feinberg and his crew of young, clueless, and ruthless executives. It's unclear whether Lee ever did, or even if he could have done more if he wanted to. Kirby, meanwhile, came to see his former partner as the author of his misery. One of his first projects for DC was the operatic Fourth World saga, which dealt with the New Gods and their adventures. One of the saga's most successful titles was *Mister Miracle*, where, in issue number 6, Kirby introduced the world to a terrible new villain.

"In the shadow world between success and failure," he wrote, "there lives the driven little man who dreams of having it all!!! The opportunistic spoiler without character or values, who preys on all things like a cannibal!!! Including you!!! Like death and taxes, we all must deal with him sometime! That's why, in this issue, we go where he lives—in the decaying antebellum grandeur of the Mockingbird Estates!!—and 'Wait for Godot' with Funky Flashman!"[9]

Flashman, of course, looked exactly like Stan Lee, a smiling man with a receding hairline who soon donned a toupee and beard to appear hipper. That he lived in a plantation and made his money by swindling and oppressing others was another blunt jab at Lee, as was the name of Flashman's sidekick—Houseroy, an allusion to Marvel writer and Lee confidant Roy Thomas, who, Kirby seemed to suggest, was some sort of house slave in Lee's exploitative estate.

Lee said nothing public about this attack or about Kirby's departure, sounding as diplomatic as he could and doing damage control whenever possible. He had no choice: he was now the key figure at the heart of a lucrative corporation owned by impatient corporate raiders, which meant more pressure than ever before. And his responsibilities, he soon realized, were shifting. Writing and editing comic books, the new bosses, unfamiliar with the industry, reasoned, was a task best left for lesser lights; Lee was famous, and he had to continue to build up his brand, which, in turn, translated into further revenue for Marvel.

Adding to all the turbulence, Lee suffered another loss when his father, Jack Lieber, died in February of 1968. The two were not close, and Lee never made any statement, publicly or otherwise, about the old man's passing, but, coming at a moment of so many transitions, Jack's death must have added to Lee's emotional turmoil. To try to chart a new course for himself, one that would take him away from merely being the face of a company he didn't control, Lee attempted to reinvent himself as something altogether new: a talk-show host.

Given the popularity of televised debate shows like *Firing Line*, and given Lee's popularity on college campuses, he pitched a producer he knew on an idea—a show in which Lee, middle-aged and goateed and besuited, would preside over a panel of radical youth, giving viewers a taste of what the kids were really up to these days.

The pilot, available online, did not go over well. Lee's guests were Jeff Shero, an editor of a popular underground newspaper; Chuck Skoro, editor of Columbia University's student newspaper; and Skip Weiss, editor of *The Daltonian*, the newspaper of Manhattan's elite prep school Dalton.

"I'm Stan Lee," the host introduced himself to an audience that might not be familiar with his creations. "I've been writing stories for the younger generation for thirty years, and . . . I have received about two to three hundred fan letters every day—probably as much as the Beatles. I spend most of my time reading the mail, and quite a lot of time answering it. I think I've learned a lot about what younger people think. More importantly, I think I've learned a lot about what young people are. Today, we've come to a time in history when there definitely is a generation gap. It seems to us that perhaps anything that can be done to bridge this gap, anything that can be done to help present the point of view of these young people . . ."

He hardly had time to finish his sentence before the mayhem began. Lee, trying to relate to his young guests, told them that as an editor himself, he tried to appeal to as large a readership as possible, embedding any political themes he wanted to address as "subliminal messages" in his comics. "I think that's an old-fashioned view," Shero replied, "because it assumes that people have power. . . . The only people that have any effect on where the country is going are people that have committed, and people who sit at the top and have the reins of power. It's only young people that are committed to changing society."

It was all downhill from there. Lee argued that law and order were important tools to keeping society intact; Shero responded that they were nothing but racist instruments designed to punish African-Americans. Lee said he believed that both "the Establishment" and the young radicals shared an interest in ending the war in Vietnam; Shero snarled and said the Establishment wanted to keep the war going for fun and profit. Lee said he saw himself as a liberal; Shero replied that there's not much difference between liberals and conservatives, and that it would take real radicalism to solve America's many systemic problems. For the first time in nearly a decade, Lee looked less like the pied piper of hip than like another aging man, rapidly losing touch with the culture. The pilot episode was the show's last.

To Marvel, however, Lee was still the Golden Goose, and rather than send him on intimate get-togethers with college kids, the company decided to book Carnegie Hall for "A Marvelous Evening with Stan Lee," advertising "An erudite evening of cataclysmic culture with your friendly neighborhood bullpen gang." The bullpen gang—John Romita, John Buscema, and others—was there, as were the journalist Tom Wolfe, wearing his signature white suit and an oversized Uncle Sam hat; the world's tallest man, the eight-foot-nine Jewish giant Eddie Carmel, who, naturally, read a poem about the Hulk; some musicians playing bad tunes; and an Australian illusionist performing magic tricks. It was such an incoherent mess that some members of the audience folded their programs into paper airplanes and hurled them on stage. The next morning, reviewers panned the evening, with one quipping that the show had all the charm of "an employer at his own Christmas party."[10]

But the critics were missing the evening's point. Together with his wife and daughter, Lee took the stage to read a poem he'd composed especially for the occasion. It was the culmination of all of his obsessions, all the sublimated stories about superheroes and their woes. It was the first—and, sadly, the last—time he would be so candid about what was truly occupying him as an artist, a stark departure from his usual deflecting and humorous approach. It was a poem about the relationship between Man and his creator. It was called "God Woke."

"God woke," the poem began,

He stretched and yawned and looked around
Haunted by a thought unfound
A vagrant thought that would not die
He rose and scanned the endless sky
He probed the is, he traced the was
He sought the yet to be
And then he found the planet Earth, the half remembered planet Earth
Steeped in pain and tragedy
And all at once he knew
He saw the world that he had wrought to suit his master plan
And then he saw the changes brought by the heedless hand of man.

God observes his creation—

> Sowing, growing, ever going
> Ever learning, never knowing
> Less than righteous, less than just
> And in the end condemned to dust

—before coming across the most terrifying sound of all. "And then," the poem continues,

> he found to his despair
> The haunting hollow sound of prayer
> A billion bodies ever bending
> A billion voices never ending.

Irate over all his creations flooding him with their petty concerns, God sinks into a long meditation about mankind, remembering their early days in the Garden of Eden and musing on the futility of their ways, their arrogance, violence, and pettiness. As the poem, more than twelve minutes long when read on stage, draws to an end, a panicky thought strikes the Almighty; what, He wonders, does the nature of Man say about the Creator? And could God himself be held accountable for Man's sins?

"The Lord, our God, could bear no more," the poem concludes,

> He looked his last at man so small
> So lately risen, so soon to fall
> He looked his last and had to know
> Whose fault this anguish, this mortal woe?
> Had man failed maker? Or maker, man?
> Who was the planner? And whose the plan?
> He looked his last then turned aside
> He knew the answer, that's why God cried.[11]

The ambiguous ending was the perfect coda for Lee's improbable decade at Marvel. His creations had struck a chord because, unlike their predecessors, they were designed not to provide answers but to provoke questions. They were deeply Jewish heroes, always quarreling, rarely certain, never submissive. Above all, they were intrigued by life's greatest mystery, the charge to go on living in a covenant with other humans who were ultimately unknowable and with a God who was ultimately unreachable. Their rights and responsibilities in this strange setting intrigued them, and even when they failed to live up to their potential—which they all did, all the time—they still couldn't imagine not trying. Theirs was rarely a comforting path—grace was for Superman and the gentiles, not Spider-Man and the Jews—but it was sustainable, and as they pursued it they grew just a little bit wiser, just a little bit more compassionate, just a little bit closer to God.

Stan Lee was fifty when he stepped off the stage at Carnegie Hall. He had recently been named Marvel's publisher—Martin Goodman had finally decided to retire—which meant writing no more comic books. Instead, he spent his days giving interviews, appearing at conventions, and otherwise feeding Marvel's mega public relations machine. From time to time, he expanded the fictional universe he had created by adding minor and largely derivative characters like the Savage She-Hulk, Bruce Banner's cousin, or Brother Voodoo, a Haitian take on Doctor Strange. Not even Jack Kirby's brief return to Marvel, in 1975, could save Lee from this rut. Eager to find new creative outlets, he looked west.

In 1981, Lee moved his family to California, where he oversaw a string of second-rate film and television projects that tried and failed to capture the Marvel magic onscreen. For the most part, he had little creative control over any of these endeavors, and he soon figured out that whatever cachet he carried in the world of comic books, it didn't quite carry over into Hollywood. In a meeting with a network executive to pitch an idea for another animated series, the VP asked Lee what he thought of the cartoons that were currently on the air. Cheerful and candid as ever, he praised them for being beautifully drawn and nicely animated, but added that the stories they told were, for the most part, dumb, and that he disliked it when cartoon characters spoke like high-pitched caricatures rather than real people. "We don't want our series to consist of talking heads," the executive said. Lee nodded and responded that he didn't mean that at all. "I'm not advocating 'talking heads,'" he clarified, "or using more dialogue. I'm only suggesting that whatever dialogue you use be better written." The executive looked straight at Lee, expressionless. "We're not looking for talking heads," she repeated.[12] It was the sort of encounter Lee would have again and again.

If he didn't understand Hollywood, he understood corporate America even less. In 1986, Marvel was sold to New World Entertainment, which in turn sold it to billionaire Ronald Perelman three years later. In the mid-1990s, investor Carl Icahn orchestrated a hostile takeover of the company, setting off a series of unfortunate events that ended with Icahn's ouster and Marvel's bankruptcy. The new owner, Toy Biz, formed a new corporate entity called Marvel Enterprises, which it sold to Disney in 2009. Throughout most of these rocky exchanges, Lee was fêted, well paid, and required to do little but meet and greet. In October of 1996, at the age of seventy-four, he stepped down as Marvel's publisher, staying on as chairman emeritus and drawing an annual salary of one million dollars.

Never one to sit idly by, Lee resolved to explore cyberspace. In 1998, he started a new Internet-based entertainment company, but it went bankrupt after his partner illegally manipulated its stocks and fled to Brazil, before being extradited to the United States and brought to justice. Lee tried a few other endeavors, but none took off. Meanwhile, his classic creations did: the X-Men starred in their first successful film adaptation in 2000, and Spider-Man got his due in 2002, both benefiting from special effects technologies that had finally caught up with Stan Lee and Jack Kirby's imaginations and visual mastery. Though Lee's contract with Marvel had guaranteed him ten percent of the profit on any future movies, he wasn't seeing a dime. This was especially galling since the Marvel movies were grossing hundreds of millions of dollars. In 2002, he sued the company, telling Bob Simon on *60 Minutes II* that he regretted having to resort to legal measures against the company that had been his home for so long. In 2005, Marvel settled, reportedly awarding Lee ten million dollars, a far cry from what he was owed but enough to satisfy his sense of fairness. The following years brought more lawsuits, and more failed pursuits, too many and too trivial to report. They also, however, brought about an onslaught of movies based on Lee's creations, arguably making his superheroes the most dominant force in American culture and fashioning his universe into what Richard Brody, writing in the *New Yorker*, termed a "secular religion."[13] Making a cameo in every Marvel movie, Lee himself became more famous than ever, this time not as a pitchman for a comic book company but as a prophet of sorts, the beatific, white-haired truth-teller whose visions of good battling evil were there to guide us through dark times. The story of how and why it happened is, in many ways, the story of America in the first decades of the twenty-first century.

12

Part of a Bigger Universe

GREAT AMERICAN ART, like all great art, flourishes primarily in times of crisis. Orson Welles, to whom Stan Lee was often compared, touched on this point when he improvised, on the set of *The Third Man*, a short speech about the conditions in which anything worthwhile might bloom. "In Italy, for thirty years, under the Borgias, they had warfare, terror, murder, and bloodshed," he quipped, "but they produced Michelangelo, Leonardo da Vinci, and the Renaissance. In Switzerland, they had brotherly love, they had five hundred years of democracy and peace, and what did that produce? The cuckoo clock."[1]

Having lived for nearly a century, Lee had seen art forms flow and ebb. He was born in the Jazz Age, just a few months after Henry van Dyke, a Princeton professor, argued in a letter that the new sound "is not music at all. It is merely an irritation of the nerves of hearing, a sensual teasing of the strings of physical passion."[2] Lee witnessed its syncopations capture the insecurities and interruptions of his first decades—the Great Depression, the Second World War and its aftermath—and then saw it ossify and become a rarefied pursuit. He heard the strumming of rock 'n' roll grow louder, more ecstatic, more orgasmic, threatening—to borrow a few words from a popular entry in the genre—to break on through to the other side. And he lived long enough to discover, along with rock's heartbroken fans, that there was no other side to break on through to, only the premature, drug-addled death that awaited its brightest stars. Like jazz, rock became a museum piece, something to ponder elegiacally while dancing to disco or swaying to pop or bopping to hip-hop. Even Hollywood, which had so sustained the young Stan, eager to escape the grim realities of his childhood, settled into a mindless groove: after a brief burst of wonder in the early 1970s—think *Jaws, The Godfather, Taxi Driver*—it wallowed in facile amusements, enamored of easy explosions and never again recapturing the glow that had made its golden age, in the 1930s and 1940s, shine so brightly. It was the same story everywhere Lee looked: an art form that had sizzled in moments of social, political, and economic cataclysms turned dull, silly, or both when prosperity struck.

The same was true of comics: by the 1990s, the readers who had loved Lee's comic books as college kids were now middle-aged men with disposable incomes, and their love for comics had hardened into a calculation informed by nostalgia and greed. With Tim Burton's *Batman* movie, released in 1989, setting off renewed interest in the art form, these adult fans took to collecting comic books, telling one another tales of rare early issues of *Superman* or *The Fantastic Four* discovered in dusty attics and fetching millions. Major auction houses soon got in on the game, as did the publishers themselves. Inflaming the market even further, Marvel, DC, and the other big houses began issuing special collectors' editions, often releasing an issue with two or three alternate covers and urging readers to buy them all. They also launched new series at an unprecedented rate, arguing that the first of anything is more likely to be valuable someday. Very few of these, of course, were worth anything, and the collecting bubble soon burst, leaving publishers and readers alike exhausted.

In this atmosphere, you might have expected Lee's creations to quietly fade away, taking their place alongside the music of trumpeter Lee Morgan, say, or the films of Ernst Lubitsch. Instead, they emerged, in their author's ninth decade, to earn nearly seven billion dollars at the box office, and to engage a new generation of fans with the old and timeless ideas Lee had spent his best years exploring. To understand why, look no further than the superhero who launched the New Wave of Marvel, Iron Man.

When the armored avenger made his cinematic debut, in May 2008, few expected him to be more than an also-ran in a field already tight with the caped, the masked, and the spectacular. This was particularly true given previous attempts to bring Lee's heroes to life onscreen: Spider-Man had just suffered a third and disastrous sequel, as had the X-Men, who disappointed fans by turning away from the dark preoccupations of the comics and toward a more flimsy focus on mindless action. The Hulk, in turn, had his terrible Hollywood moment as well, tamed by art house director Ang Lee into a brooding soul with oedipal overtones. Any astute reader of comics, however, might have seen these mishaps coming. It was one thing to dash off a new story line each month in a medium that cost little to produce and less to consume; it was another thing altogether to keep a franchise of multimillion-dollar pictures going and to find fresh story lines that engaged both diehard fans and newcomers. Those early Marvel films followed the same pattern, launching with a coherent and compelling first movie focused on the character's origin story, then delivering a second installment that was slightly darker and featured some of the hero's most celebrated enemies before running out of steam with movie number three, which, in most cases, was just a mindless tangle of loud action sequences. This predicament is why the Spider-Man franchise, for example, was rebooted ten years after it first appeared on the big screen, and then again five years after that, each relaunch benefiting from the depth and duration of Lee's original stories and ideas. But delivering the same ancient creation myth in slight variation every other year was hardly a sustainable business model, which is why Marvel realized it needed a different approach. Thankfully, it looked to Lee for inspiration.

Displeased with merely licensing its characters to other studios, Marvel formed its own, securing $525 million in credit from Merrill Lynch, largely on the strength of the enduring popularity of Lee's work. The new enterprise was headed by Kevin Feige, a thirty-three-year-old comic book fanboy who had read enough of Lee and Kirby to realize that the path to success lay in emulating everything they had done. First, he resolved to pick up Lee's vision of Marvel as a cohesive cosmos of characters. Rather than release a string of independent movies, Feige announced an ambitious plan for the creation of what he called the Marvel Cinematic Universe, a series of intertwined movies that would operate just as Lee and Kirby's comics had. Some movies would introduce new characters, others would continue ongoing story lines, and all would feature guest appearances, allusions, and other reminders that the Marvel mythology occupies one unified world. Just as Lee and Kirby introduced the Black Panther, for example, in *The Fantastic Four* only to have him join the Avengers before receiving his own comic book, the Marvel Cinematic Universe—or MCU, as it is more commonly known—first hinted at the arrival of the character in 2010's *Iron Man 2*, introduced him in a minor role in *Captain America: Civil War* in 2016, and launched his own movie in

February 2018 before having him appear, later that year, in the latest *Avengers* movie.

To make sure that MCU was protected from the capricious impulses of studio executives, the same species that had so frustrated Lee himself years earlier, Feige convened a committee of nerds, including a handful of Marvel's senior comic book writers, to help steer things in the right direction. He also adopted his own version of Lee's Marvel Method, giving the artists he selected to direct his films an uncommon degree of freedom and creative control. "The most simple way I could put it is Marvel doesn't come to the filmmakers and say, 'Here's what the next movie is,'" explained Anthony Russo, who directed several of the MCU's most successful entries. "They come to the filmmakers and say, 'What is the next movie?' That's very much the process."[3] With these principles in place, Marvel soon thrived onscreen as it once had on the page. And just as it had been under Kirby and Lee, it was once again seen as the sandbox to which a nation undergoing a social and political sea change retreated to work out its deepest moral quandaries.

It's no accident that it was Iron Man who was chosen to lead the charge and set MCU in motion. Created by Lee in 1963, he was always meant as a sort of a dare. "It was the height of the Cold War," Lee recalled in an interview included with the movie's DVD release. "The readers, the young readers, if there was one thing they hated, it was war, it was the military. . . . So I got a hero who represented that to the hundredth degree. He was a weapons manufacturer, he was providing weapons for the army, he was rich, he was an industrialist. . . . I thought it would be fun to take the kind of character that nobody would like, none of our readers would like, and shove him down their throats and make them like him."

It worked, which taught Lee two important lessons. The first was that artists had no other choice—indeed, no other obligation—but to refuse the pieties of their time, even if the latter dressed up in the hip garb of the young and claimed themselves to be unimpeachably moral, enlightened, and just. Sure, the college kids were antiwar, but to follow their lead, to pretend that the only approved approach to something as fundamentally human as war was to roll the eyes and repeat a few righteous slogans, meant giving up an opportunity to ask precisely the sort of questions a nation embroiled in violent conflict ought to ask. Lee was enough of a master publicist to realize the value of riding the coattails of outrage culture, but also enough of an artist to know that timeless stories were rooted in sturdier soil than the quicksand of political posturing.

The second lesson Lee had learned from Iron Man's success is that the best way to tell stories is to tell them again. A wealthy industrialist who discovers the limits of his inventions, a cad whose heart literally breaks—it's repaired by the atomic generator that powers his mighty suit—and who must learn to make and keep friends, Iron Man and his alter ego Tony Stark are just another variation on Bruce Banner and the Hulk, another pair of Adam the First and Adam the Second grappling with loneliness and faith.

When he first emerged on the scene, Iron Man was there to tell a divided America that it was looking at the world all wrong. Those who cheered for armed interventions were invited to witness the brokenness of Tony Stark, who, despite championing their values, was no closer to virtue; later in the series, he became the first Marvel character to succumb to alcoholism, a warning that unchecked reliance on the proud self could end only in disaster. On the other end of the ideological divide, those who preached peace and love still had to wrestle with the glory of Iron Man, who championed the oppressed and proved, in one adventure after another, the inconvenient truth that keeping the peace often calls for strong arms. And both camps had to reckon with the comic's larger theme, the call to a covenantal community: to survive, Stark has no choice but to reveal his secret identity as Iron Man to a small coterie of confidants, and it's this circle of intimates, much more than the advanced military machinery at his disposal, that gives him the power to persist.

This was no mere flowery call to get along with those who thought differently. It was a stern reminder, drawn from the core of Jewish theology, that redemption comes only when human beings get together and pursue common goals, even if—or especially when—they couldn't make much sense of existence. It's the same sentiment that Leonard Cohen, writing years later, captured in his song "Anthem" when he advised us to "Ring the bells that still can ring/Forget your perfect offering/There is a crack in everything/That's how the light gets in."[4] Rather than await some redeemer—either a conquering general or a healing emissary of love—to swoop down and deliver us, Judaism guides us to focus on our relationship with one another and with God, the only recipe for a society designed for the long haul. Iron Man is there to deliver the message, and in 1963, the beginning of the great fracture that would tear American society apart for decades to come, it was just the message the nation needed to hear.

We needed to hear it again in 2008. Our communications technologies, the platforms on which we shared our national stories and forged our collective identity, were changing rapidly. Rather than be tethered to one another by a network of national media outlets—comic books, television stations, newspapers— we were now plugged into the World Wide Web, which meant that we could find meaning and affinities with people who weren't necessarily our neighbors and who didn't share our specific life experiences. We were free, even encouraged, to see ourselves less as Americans and more as global citizens, at liberty to create cultural enclaves we shared with like-minded people wherever they happened to live. This shift wasn't unprecedented—the printing press, for example, had brought similar upheaval, making it possible to communicate with people in faraway corners of each country and, as a result, giving rise to nationalism—but the potency of the technology was, and it didn't take long for the bonds that once tied Americans to one another to grow slack.

Rather than fight over the soul of the nation, as they had done so many times before, Americans were now breaking apart into two distinct camps, defined by the British journalist David Goodhart as the Anywheres and the Somewheres. The former were the educated and urban crowds who could practice their professions—law, medicine, graphic design—in any corner of the globe, and who therefore felt closer to their peers in Berlin or London than they did to their cousins in Iowa or Tennessee. The latter were blue-collar workers who watched with dismay as so much of the economy went global, which meant that the lives they cherished, lives rooted in their hometowns and their extended families and their time-honored traditions, were now considered antiquated and impractical in the new world order. This wasn't just the same old conflict between the moderns and the fundamentalists: The two groups weren't at war for the future of a nation both saw as the cornerstone of their identity. Instead, they were tribes apart, each seeing the other as alien. The Somewheres still considered themselves beholden to the idea of the nation-state, while the Anywheres were beginning to feel that there were other, larger, more rewarding groups to be a part of, the largest of which being the entirety of the human race.

With little to agree on and with no shared vision of the future, these two groups rapidly lost their faith in the nation's institutions, as those, by definition, require a modicum of consensus to function. Trust—in government, in academia, in the press—plummeted, and rhetoric grew more heated, fanned by social media networks that pushed us to create our own small echo chambers that amplified none but the voices with which we already agreed. This, naturally, made politics, the pursuit of compromise, much harder to practice, which, in turn, left us yearning for an inspirational leader who could bring about transformation and save us all. In 2008, with a winning campaign that struck a metaphysical note when it invoked hope and change, that man was Barack Obama.

The forty-fourth president enjoyed riffing on the theme of himself as savior. "Contrary to the rumors you have heard, I was not born in a manger," he told the beaming crowd gathered at a fundraising dinner in New York. "I was actually born on Krypton and sent here by my father, Jor-El, to save the planet Earth."[5] DC Comics took the joke literally, and, a year later, published a Superman reboot in which the Man of Steel ends up not as the meek and mild-mannered Clark Kent but as an African-American politician named Calvin Ellis who ends up being president.

The Superman theory of history, however, was precisely what Stan Lee had spent his career warning us against. Every one of his creations exists to remind us that no one man or woman, no matter how smart or well meaning or brave, could carry the world's weight on his or her shoulders. Real heroes stand out not because they have no flaws—at the same dinner, Obama joked, "If I had to name my greatest strength, I guess it would be my humility. Greatest weakness, it's possible I may be too awesome"—but because they are ready to face them.[6]

Predating Obama's election by six months, Iron Man was an alternative to most of mainstream culture the moment he took his first onscreen flight. It's a funny thing to say, maybe, about a movie that ended up making more than $318 million, but nothing about the film's spirit was recognizable elsewhere in the zeitgeist of 2008. Its fellow box-office smashers—Batman of *The Dark Knight*, the vampires and werewolves of *Twilight*, and Hancock, Will Smith's immortal superhero—were all studies in essentialism, revolving around heroes who were loved, loathed,

and feared because of a fundamental identity they could neither control nor change. These heroes made a mint because
they suggested that progress could be achieved not by trying to
find common ground—an impossibility in a reality shaped by
divisive media technologies—but by an ongoing struggle for
power, waged by unchanging and unchangeable individuals
and groups and justified by vague ideological affiliations. This
is why *The Dark Knight*, for example, revolves almost entirely
around superheroes and supervillains staging big, public spec-
tacles, the latter hoping to extinguish the citizens' hopes for the
future and the former fighting to preserve them.

Iron Man was cut from a different sheet of metal. Unlike
any of his contemporaries in the superhero class of 2008, he
wasn't interested in dichotomies like good versus evil or powerful versus powerless. To him, these were preoccupations that
kept us from addressing the real challenge each of us faced, the
challenge of learning to step up and stand up for one another,
the test Cain flunked and Abraham aced and every Stan Lee
character contemplated furiously. Think like Batman, went the
film's logic, and you're just another mirthless partisan in a war
that cherishes grand abstractions like justice at the expense of
real people, which is why so many innocents had to die in *The
Dark Knight* for the somber plot to make any sense. Think like
Tony Stark, and you're engaged in the messy, imperfect, and
absolutely sacred business of living life to the fullest.

As the first Iron Man movie draws to an end, in a midcred-
its scene, Tony Stark meets Nick Fury, the head of a special secret agency entrusted with protecting the world from threats.
"Mr. Stark," Fury informs the bewildered entrepreneur, "you've
become part of a bigger universe."[7] The extent of this universe
became better known with each additional film released, introducing audiences to Thor, Captain America, the Avengers, Ant-
Man, Doctor Strange, the Guardians of the Galaxy, and the
Black Panther. And while these heroes varied wildly—in tone,

in style, in preoccupations—they shared the same fundamental belief in community, accountability, responsibility, and compassion.

Few others did, onscreen or off. As the Marvel Cinematic Universe flourished, American culture was growing nastier, more brutish and short-tempered. Reality TV favored the gleefully mean, as did Twitter. Cable news thrived on controversies, real or otherwise. Increasingly, Americans of all stripes imagined themselves as combatants, and saw every aspect of life as a battlefield. The MCU acknowledged these tensions—several of its most successful titles revolve around the heroes engaged in precisely the sort of ugly clashes on display every day anywhere from Congress to Fox News—but it also showed viewers a way out. If Captain America and Iron Man, two proud and powerful hotheads, could realize that they both served a bigger cause and put their considerable differences aside, maybe, the MCU seemed to suggest, so could America's partisans. And if said partisans wanted a lesson in community building, all they had to do was pay attention to the MCU's voice, the voice crafted decades earlier by Stan Lee, a voice that was funny, playful, warm, and mesmerized, like a precocious child, by the big, eternal questions of being.

Some dull critics mistook this childlike wonder for childishness, a dimwitted error in judgment that had plagued comic books from the very first. Lee knew better. America, he realized, was a youthful and excitable nation, and its art was best when it mirrored its wild ambitions and indiscretions. Not for Americans was the scolding delivered daily by pundits and politicians right and left, or the sermonizing by professors and experts, or the insistence by the self-appointed mandarins of culture that this entry or that was offensive, inappropriate, or unacceptable. Americans liked their stories, liked their music and their imaginations, to be free and unfettered, going wherever they pleased, borrowing whatever they fancied. And they needed these stories to end with an affirmation of the we, a rededication to the crazy project of the only nation in human history that came together solely to defend its citizens' right to be happy. That was the spirit animating the American classics Lee enjoyed as a child, the spirit of Errol Flynn and Mark Twain. And now that America was more divided than ever before, it turned to the same spirit, this time embodied by Lee and his creations, to help it through yet another moment of social upheaval.

Contemplating his own role within this new age of Marvel, Lee had one final insight. Now an old man, he realized that the universe he had created was mature enough to stand on its own. It no longer needed Stan the Man to shape it or sell it. It no longer needed to be defended against the snobs who considered it lowbrow—it was making enough money to dwarf them all. Marvel was no longer the counterculture. It was now the culture itself.

Armed with that insight, Lee began his long walk into the sunset. He was there, onscreen, in most Marvel movies, but only for a brief moment, and usually as some minor and confused character, like an old man trying to tow away Thor's immovable hammer in his pickup truck or a guy at a red carpet event Tony Stark mistakes for Hugh Hefner. These appearances were designed as inside jokes, each a wink to those in the know, a page from the old Merry Marvel Marching Society playbook that reassured fans that even though they were watching some bigbudget commercial movie produced by a crew of hundreds and costing tens of millions of dollars to make, their old friendly neighborhood comic book writer Stan Lee was still milling about, inviting them to stop by, say hello, and ask a question or two.

These onscreen cameos infused the films with the same sense of freewheeling joy that had made the comic books so successful. They also helped Lee, ever the master of public relations, maintain control of his own legacy, even as his twilight years grew darker. Joan passed away after suffering a stroke at age ninety-five in 2017, a few months shy of the couple's seventieth wedding anniversary. Her death rattled Lee. Rather than reflect on it, he reacted in the only way that ever made sense to him, by throwing himself into more professional obligations. Despite being ninety-four, in frail health, and under doctor's orders not to fly for more than two hours at a time, Lee committed to a long string of appearances in conferences for comic book fans, now a lucrative industry. On panel after panel, he delivered the same persona that had so entertained for so long: a bit raspy-voiced, a bit slower, but charming and always ready with a quip or a story about the good old days of Marvel.

But this hectic pace was not sustainable for a man his age, and Lee's life soon fell into chaos. News reports started circulating, each more troubling than the last: a former manager was suspected of attempting to control Lee and siphon off some of his considerable funds, leading his daughter to file an elder-abuse restraining order and win back Lee's control over his finances. A nurse working for Lee claimed that he had groped her and exposed himself to her. A former business partner stole a few vials containing Lee's blood, selling them to fans as the ultimate Marvel collectible. These allegations and tribulations did little to tarnish Lee's image. His onscreen cameos kept on coming— he recorded a number in advance—which meant that even as Stan Lee the person got frail and sick, Stan Lee the character joined Spider-Man and Iron Man and Thor and the Hulk and the rest of his creations onscreen, where they will all live for as long as people are interested in making sense of their own powers, of each other, and of God.

Lee died on November 12, 2018, of congestive heart failure. He was ninety-five. Almost immediately, the Internet lit up with farewells, with nearly every actor who has ever appeared in a Marvel movie sharing her or his memories of the genial Lee. Others, like Paul McCartney or Lin-Manuel Miranda, soon followed suit, expressing their admiration for Lee and his work.

Even New York City joined in on the tributes, naming Lee's old block in the Bronx after him. Just as ubiquitous were the old quibbles, with some taking the opportunity to argue, once again, that Lee was nothing but a clever manipulator of other people's talent, rising on the backs of geniuses like Steve Ditko and Jack Kirby. Anyone reading through the entirety of the encomia and the detractions, however, would still have been hard pressed to come up with anything resembling a real human being. Even those who were close to him failed to offer more than a handful of anecdotes that would shed light on what sort of person Lee really was, and even those anecdotes often sounded like the sort of tongue-in-cheek, vaguely self-aggrandizing tales Lee had been telling about himself since he was a young boy. Lee died as he had lived, a solitary figure surrounded by too many adjectives, a creator of myths who could be understood only as another character in his fictional universe.

How, then, should we remember him? One moment in particular comes to mind. It's one of his beloved cameos, predating the official launch of the Marvel Cinematic Universe and coming in the middle of 2007's *Spider-Man 3*. Peter Parker, played by Tobey Maguire, is walking through Times Square when a headline flashing on a ticker overhead catches his eye. "Spider-Man to receive key to the city," it reads, and Parker, amused, stops to look at it. Stan Lee walks into the frame, stands alongside Parker, and takes a moment to read the news as well. "You know," he says before putting his hand on Parker's shoulder and disappearing into the crowd, "I guess one person can make a difference. 'Nuff said."[8]

—————

1. So What's the Risk?

1. Quoted in Sean Howe, *Marvel Comics: The Untold Story* (New York: Harper Perennial, 2012), 30.

2. Quoted in David Hajdu, *The Ten-Cent Plague: The Great Comic-Book Scare and How It Changed America* (New York: Picador, 2009), 327.

3. Quoted in Roy Thomas and Jim Amash, "To Keep Busy as a Freelancer, You Should Have Three Accounts," *Alter Ego*, December 2003.

4. Quoted in Stan Lee, Peter David, and Colleen Doran, *Amazing Fantastic Incredible: A Marvelous Memoir* (New York: Touchstone, 2015).

5. Stan Lee, in *Fantastic Four* documentary, production year and director unknown.

2. Stan Lee Is God

1. Stan Lee and George Mair, *Excelsior! The Amazing Life of Stan Lee* (New York: Fireside, 2002), 10.

2. *The Edgar Bergen and Charlie McCarthy Show*, Onesmedia, 2012.

3. Caroline Bird, *The Invisible Scar* (New York: Longman, 1978), 59.

4. William Kelley Wright, "The Recovery of the Religious Sentiment," in *Contemporary American Theology: Theological Autobiographies*, ed. Vergilius Fern (New York: Round Table, 1933), 341–76.

5. Hornell Hart, "Changing Social Attitudes and Interests," in *Recent Social Trends* 1 (1933): 382–443.

6. Jordan Raphael and Tom Spurgeon, *Stan Lee and the Rise and Fall of the American Comic Book* (Chicago: Chicago Review Press, 2004), 6–7.

7. Ibid., 5.

8. Quoted in Timothy Corrigan, *The Essay Film: From Montaigne, After Marker* (Oxford: Oxford University Press, 2011), 123.

9. Quoted in Sean Howe, *Marvel Comics: The Untold Story* (New York: Harper Perennial, 2012), 19.

10. Ibid., 10.

11. Jim Amash, "Simon Says," *Alter Ego*, March 2008.

12. Quoted in David Hajdu, *The Ten-Cent Plague: The Great Comic-Book Scare and How It Changed America* (New York: Picador, 2009), 21.

13. Quoted in Arie Kaplan, *From Krakow to Krypton: Jews and Comic Books* (Philadelphia: Jewish Publication Society, 2008), 3.

14. Ibid., 4.

15. Quoted in Hajdu, *The Ten-Cent Plague*, 21.

16. Quoted in Arie Kaplan, "Kings of Comics: How Jews Created the Comic Book Industry, Part I: The Golden Age (1933–1955)," in *Reform Judaism* 32, no. 1 (2003).

17. Quoted in Kaplan, *From Krakow to Krypton*, 8.

18. Hajdu, *The Ten-Cent Plague*, 30.

3. Getting in the Way

1. *Captain America*, no. 1 (1941).

2. Russell D. Buhite and David W. Levy, *FDR's Fireside Chats* (Norman: University of Oklahoma Press, 1992), 162.

3. Quoted in Bradford W. Wright, *Comic Book Nation: The Transformation of Youth Culture in America* (Baltimore: Johns Hopkins University Press, 2003), 36.

4. *Captain America*, no. 3 (1941).

5. *Superman: Red Son*, no. 1 (2003).

6. *Captain America*, no. 2 (1941).

7. Quoted in Harry Brod, *Superman Is Jewish? How Comic Book Superheroes Came to Serve Truth, Justice, and the Jewish-American Way* (New York: Free Press, 2016).

8. Tractate Shabbat 63a.

9. Michael Walzer, *Exodus and Revolution* (New York: Basic, 1986).

10. "Stan Lee Speaks at the 1975 San Diego Comic-Con Convention," YouTube, uploaded January 6, 2010, https://www.youtube.com/watch?v=MhJuBqDTM9Q.

11. *U.S.A. Comics*, no. 1 (1941).

12. Cited in David Hajdu, *The Ten-Cent Plague: The Great Comic-Book Scare and How It Changed America* (New York: Picador, 2009), 44–45.

13. Quoted in Sean Howe, *Marvel Comics: The Untold Story* (New York: Harper Perennial, 2012), 23.

14. Ibid.

15. Quoted in Bob Batchelor, *Stan Lee: The Man Behind Marvel* (Lanham, MD: Rowman and Littlefield, 2017), 28–29.

16. Ibid., 29.

17. Ibid.

18. Quoted in Howe, *Marvel Comics*, 23.

4. Playwright

1. Danny Fingeroth, *A Marvelous Life: The Amazing Story of Stan Lee* (New York: St. Martin's, 2019), location 36.

2. Ibid., 24.

3. Stan Lee, "Comic Relief: Comic Books Aren't Just for Entertainment," *Edutopia*, August 11, 2005.

4. Stan Lee and George Mair, *Excelsior! The Amazing Life of Stan Lee* (New York: Fireside, 2002), 43–44.

5. David Anthony Kraft, "The Foom Interview: Stan Lee," *Foom*, March 1977.

6. *All Winners Comics*, no. 19 (1946).

7. "Number of TV Households in America," http://www .buffalohistory.org/Explore/Exhibits/virtual_exhibits/wheels_of _power/educ_materials/television_handout.pdf.

8. Jim Amash, "I Did Better on Bulletman than I Did on Millie the Model," in *Alter Ego*, December 2005.

9. Lee and Mair, *Excelsior!*

10. *Secrets Behind the Comics*, no. 1 (1947).

11. Quoted in David Hajdu, *The Ten-Cent Plague: The Great Comic-Book Scare and How It Changed America* (New York: Picador, 2009), 75.

12. Quoted ibid., 99.

13. Ibid., 101.

14. Philip Quarles, "Senate Subcommittee on Juvenile Delinquency: Wertham Versus Gaines on Decency Standards," WNYC New York Public Radio, https://www.wnyc.org/story /215975-senate-subcommittee-juvenile-delinquency-ii/.

15. Quoted in Hajdu, *The Ten-Cent Plague*, 290.

16. *Suspense*, no. 29 (1953).

5. The World's Greatest Comic Magazine!

1. John Romita, "Face Front, True Believers! The Comics Industry Sounds Off on Stan Lee," *Comics Journal*, October 1995, 83.

2. *The Fantastic Four*, no. 1 (1961).

3. Ibid.

4. *The Fantastic Four* 3, no. 56 (2002).

5. Quoted in Robert Pinsky, *The Life of David* (New York: Schocken, 2008), 2.

6. *Fantastic Four* no. 1.

7. Zvi Mark, "Dybbuk and Devekut in the Shivhe ha-Besht: Toward a Phenomenology of Madness in Early Hasidism," in *Spirit Possessions in Judaism: Cases and Contexts from the Middle Ages to the Present*, ed. Matt Goldish (Detroit: Wayne University Press, 2003), 269.

8. *Fantastic Four* no. 1.

9. Ibid.

10. *The Fantastic Four*, no. 7 (1962).

11. Quoted in Ian MacDonald, *Revolution in the Head: The Beatles' Records and the Sixties* (Chicago: Chicago Review Press, 2007), 191.

12. Jeffrey J. Kripal, *Mutants and Mystics: Science Fiction, Superhero Comics, and the Paranormal* (Chicago: University of Chicago Press, 2011), 286–87.

6. I Don't Need You!

1. Stan Lee and George Mair, *Excelsior! The Amazing Life of Stan Lee* (New York: Fireside, 2002), 120.

2. *The Incredible Hulk*, no. 1.

3. Ibid.

4. Ibid.

5. Lee and Mair, *Excelsior!* 122.

6. Genesis 1:27–28.

7. Joseph B. Soloveitchik, *The Lonely Man of Faith* (New York: Image, 2006), 17.

8. Ibid., 19.

9. Ecclesiastes 4:9.

10. Genesis 2:7–24.

11. Soloveitchik, *Lonely Man of Faith*.

12. *Incredible Hulk* no. 1.

13. Ibid.

14. Sean Howe, *Marvel Comics: The Untold Story* (New York: Harper Perennial, 2012).

15. Roslyn Davis, Roslyn Reports, *South Shore Record*, July 4, 1963, quoted in Danny Fingeroth, *A Marvelous Life: The Amazing*

Story of Stan Lee (New York: St. Martin's, 2019), location 149. The painter Davis mentions is obviously David Manzur of Colombia.

16. Quoted in Howe, *Marvel Comics*, 4.

7. With Great Power

1. Don Thrasher, "Stan Lee's Secret to Success: A Marvelous Imagination," *Dayton Daily News*, January 21, 2006.

2. Stan Lee and George Mair, *Excelsior! The Amazing Life of Stan Lee* (New York: Fireside, 2002), 126.

3. Quoted in Roy Thomas, *Alter Ego: The Comic Book Artist Collection* (Raleigh, NC: TwoMorrows, 2001).

4. *Amazing Fantasy*, no. 15 (1962).

5. Ibid.

6. Ibid.

7. Ibid.

8. Luke 12:48.

9. Winston Churchill, speech to the House of Commons, February 28, 1906.

10. Franklin Delano Roosevelt, draft of Jefferson Day address, April 1945.

11. Genesis 4:5–7.

12. Joseph B. Soloveitchik, *Chumash Mesoras Harav: Sefer Bereishis* (New York: OU Press, 2013), 36.

13. Genesis 4:13.

14. Quoted in Lee and Mair, *Excelsior!*, 128.

15. *The Amazing Spider-Man*, no. 1 (1963).

16. Genesis 4:9.

17. Genesis 4:10.

18. Genesis 4:12.

19. *The Amazing Spider-Man*, no. 4 (1963).

20. *The Amazing Spider-Man*, no. 3 (1963).

21. Alan Moore, quoted in Jonathan Ross, *In Search of Steve Ditko*. BBC4, 2007.

22. *The Amazing Spider-Man*, no. 6 (1963).

23. Roy Thomas, "Stan Lee's Amazing Marvel Interview!" *Alter Ego*, August 2011, 7.

24. Quoted in Tom DeFalco, *Comics Creators on Spider-Man* (London: Titan, 2004), 29–30.

25. Stan Lee, *Origins of Marvel Comics* (New York: Marvel, 1997), 164.

8. We Only Fight in Self-Defense!

1. *X-Men*, no. 1 (1963).

2. *X-Men*, no. 5 (1964).

3. *X-Men*, no. 4 (1964).

4. Quoted in Brian Cronin, *100 Things X-Men Fans Should Know and Do Before They Die* (Chicago: Triumph, 2018).

5. Theodore Bikel, "A Farewell to SNCC," *Tablet*, August 16, 2016.

6. *X-Men*, no. 16 (1966).

7. Danny Fingeroth, *Disguised as Clark Kent: Jews, Comics, and the Creation of the Superhero* (New York: Continuum, 2007), 118.

8. *X-Men*, no. 13 (1965).

9. *X-Men* 4.

10. Ibid.

11. Quoted in Arie Kaplan, "Kings of Comics: How Jews Created the Comic Book Industry," *Reform Judaism* 32, no. 2 (2003).

12. Ibid.

13. *X-Men*, 2, no. 1 (1991).

14. *X-Men* 4.

15. See Mark Alexander, "Lee & Kirby: The Wonder Years," *The Jack Kirby Collector* 18, no. 58 (2011): 1–31.

9. Face Front!

1. Quoted in Bob Batchelor, *Stan Lee: The Man Behind Marvel* (Lanham, MD: Rowman and Littlefield, 2017), 111.

2. *Fantastic Four*, no. 45 (1965).

3. Jonathan Lethem, "Izations," *The Ecstasy of Influence* (New York: Vintage, 2012), 151–59.

4. Ralph Young, *Dissent: The History of an American Idea* (New York: New York University Press, 2015), 445.

5. Stan Lee and George Mair, *Excelsior! The Amazing Life of Stan Lee* (New York: Fireside, 2002), 162.

6. Stan Lee, *Stan's Soapbox: The Collection* (Los Angeles: The Hero Initiative, 2008), 7.

7. Ibid., 18.

8. Quoted in Sean Howe, *Marvel Comics: The Untold Story* (New York: Harper Perennial, 2012), 56.

9. Stan Lee at Princeton, 1966, available on YouTube at https://www.youtube.com/watch?v=A73KehrmpOU.

10. Sally Kempton, "Spider-Man's Dilemma: Super-Anti-Hero in Forest Hills," *The Village Voice*, April 1, 1965.

11. Michael McClure, *The Beard* (New York: Grove, 1967).

12. Quoted in Jeff McLaughlin, ed., *Stan Lee: Conversations* (Jackson: University Press of Mississippi, 2007), 14–19.

13. Daniel Raim, "Marvel Mon Amour: Stan Lee and Alain Resnais's Unmade Monster Movie," The Criterion Collection, https://www.criterion.com/current/posts/5418-marvel-mon-amour -stan-lee-and-alain-resnais-s-unmade-monster-movie.

14. Lee and Mair, *Excelsior!*, 141–42.

15. Nat Freedland, "Super Heroes with Super Problems," *New York Herald Tribune Sunday Magazine*, January 9, 1966.

16. Quoted in Howe, *Marvel Comics*, 65.

10. My Own Power Has Never Been Fully Tested!

1. Quoted in Mark Evanier, *Kirby: King of Comics* (New York: Abrams ComicArts, 2008), 145.

2. Numbers 13:33.

3. *Fantastic Four*, no. 49 (1966).

4. Ibid.

5. Ibid.

6. Ibid.

7. Ibid.

8. Ibid.

9. Babylonian Talmud, Bava Metzia, 59b.

10. *Fantastic Four* no. 49.

11. Ibid.

12. Ibid.

13. *Fantastic Four,* no. 50 (1966).

14. Ibid.

15. Ibid.

16. Ibid.

17. Genesis 18:23–24.

18. Susan Neiman, *Moral Clarity: A Guide for Grown-Up Idealists* (Princeton: Princeton University Press, 2009), 10.

19. Søren Kierkegaard, *Fear and Trembling* (Cambridge: Cambridge University Press, 2006).

20. *Fantastic Four* no. 50.

21. Quoted in Sean Howe, *Marvel Comics: The Untold Story* (New York: Harper Perennial, 2012), 73.

22. *Fantastic Four,* no. 72 (1968).

23. Quoted in Evanier, *Kirby,* 151.

24. Leslie Raddatz, "Banker with a Sting," *TV Guide,* October 29, 1966.

11. This Long-Awaited Leap

1. Stan Lee, *Stan's Soapbox: The Collection* (Los Angeles: The Hero Initiative, 2008), 13.

2. Quoted in Sean Howe, *Marvel Comics: The Untold Story* (New York: Harper Perennial, 2012), 80.

3. Ibid.

4. Stan Lee and Jack Kirby, *Not Brand Echh,* no. 1 (1967).

5. Quoted in Howe, *Marvel Comics,* 96.

6. *The Amazing Spider-Man,* no. 68 (1969).

7. Otto Friedrich, *Decline and Fall* (New York: Harper and Row, 1970), 320.

8. Stan Lee and George Mair, *Excelsior! The Amazing Life of Stan Lee* (New York: Fireside, 2002), 179–80.

9. *Mister Miracle,* no. 6.

10. "Comics Come to Carnegie," *New York Post,* January 6, 1972.

11. Stan Lee, "God Woke," available online at https://www.youtube.com/watch?v=t-z79V58YuE.

12. Lee and Mair, *Excelsior!*, 207–8.

13. Richard Brody, "The Superhero Movie as Secular Religion," *New Yorker*, December 29, 2018.

12. Part of a Bigger Universe

1. Carol Reed, dir., *The Third Man* (London Films, 1949).

2. Quoted in Karl Koenig, ed., *Jazz in Print: 1859–1929* (Hillsdale, NY: Pendragon, 2002), 154.

3. Haleigh Foutch, "The Russo Brothers on What It Takes to Land a Marvel Directing Gig," *Collider*, April 30, 2016, http://collider.com/russo-brothers-captain-america-civil-war-interview/.

4. Leonard Cohen, "Anthem," *The Future* (New York: Columbia Records, 1992).

5. Quoted in Mark Mooney, "McCain, Obama Trade Campaign Attacks for Late-Night Jokes," *ABC News*, October 17, 2008.

6. Ibid.

7. Jon Favreau, dir., *Iron Man* (Paramount Pictures, 2008).

8. Sam Raimi, dir., *Spider-Man 3* (Columbia Pictures, 2007).

ACKNOWLEDGMENTS

Book-writing, like crime-fighting or web-slinging or hammer-swinging, is a lonely job that is worth a damn only if you're fortunate enough to enjoy the support of a community of friends, family members, and colleagues, and few have been as fortunate as me.

First, I wish to thank the wise David Mikics, who suggested that I turn my obsession with Stan Lee and his creations, which began when I was barely old enough to read, into a more formal meditation.

Once the idea was set in motion, I was privileged to find a home with the Yale Jewish Lives series, an inimitably inspired publishing endeavor I have always loved passionately. I am thankful to Leon Black for his support and generosity, and for the series' entire team. I am particularly grateful to Heather Gold for her judicious and patient shepherding of this book, and to the great Ileene Smith for having faith in me and for making this book so much better with her insightful edits. To Dan Heaton, whose wisdom, humor, and warmth made this a far richer book, I am endlessly grateful.

As always, I would not be able to achieve much of any writerly merit without my dear friend and agent, the incomparable Anne Edelstein. Nor would I have had much success thinking my way through the thicket of Jewish history and ideas had it not been my exceedingly good luck to be a part of *Tablet* magazine, my emotional, intellectual, and spiritual home. To my good friends there—Alana Newhouse, David Samuels, Wayne Hoffman, Matthew Fishbane, Gabriel Sanders, Jacob Siegel, Marjorie Ingall, Armin Rosen, and Yair Rosenberg—I am thrilled to have the opportunity to learn from you each day and so grateful for your brilliance, your dedication, your spirit, and your cheer.

Four years ago, I was reluctantly talked into what soon turned out to be one of the most rewarding experiences of my life: Unorthodox, a podcast as curious and irreverent and warm and funny and accepting as Jewish life at its very best ought to be. To my dear, dear friends and partners in this adventure—Stephanie Butnick, Mark Oppenheimer, Josh Kross, and Sara Fredman-Aeder—may we never run out of things to argue about.

To my mother, Iris Mindlin, for her faith and support, I am deeply thankful. And finally, as ever, to my family, my own small band of heroes who save me always and from everything: To Lisa Ann Sandell, the love of my life, and to our beautiful children, Lily Bess and Hudson Siegfried, you are, and will always be, my marvels.

INDEX

JEWISH LIVES is a prizewinning series of interpretative biography designed to explore the many facets of Jewish identity. Individual volumes illuminate the imprint of Jewish figures upon literature, religion, philosophy, politics, cultural and economic life, and the arts and sciences. Subjects are paired with authors to elicit lively, deeply informed books that explore the range and depth of the Jewish experience from antiquity to the present.

Jewish Lives is a partnership of Yale University Press and the Leon D. Black Foundation. Ileene Smith is editorial director. Anita Shapira and Steven J. Zipperstein are series editors.